Mastering

THE

SYCHOLOGY
OF GOLF
WITH
EMOTIONAL
CORE
THERAPY

Robert Moylan

ISBN: 1507700105

ISBN 13: 9781507700105

Library of Congress Control Number: 2015901409

CreateSpace Independent Publishing Platform,

North Charleston, South Carolina

CONTENTS

DISCLAIMER

This book details the author's personal experiences with and opinions about mental health and relationships. The author and publisher are providing this book and its contents on an "as is" basis and make no representations or warranties of any kind with respect to this book or its contents. The author and publisher disclaim all such representations and warranties of merchantability and healthcare for a particular purpose. In addition, the author and publisher do not represent or warrant that the information accessible via this book is accurate, complete, or current.

The statements made in this book are not intended to diagnose, treat, cure, or prevent any specific condition or illness. Please consult with your own physician or mental healthcare provider regarding the suggestions and recommendations made in this book.

Neither the author nor the publisher will be liable for any damages arising out of, or in connection with the use of this book. This is a comprehensive limitation of liability that applies to damages of any kind, including (without limitation): compensatory, direct, indirect, or consequential damages; loss of data, income or profit, loss of or damage to property and claims of third parties.

You understand that this book is not intended as a substitute for consultation with a licensed healthcare practitioner, such as your physician or therapist. Before you begin any healthcare program or change your lifestyle in any way, you will consult with your physician or healthcare provider to ensure that you are in good health and that the examples used in this book will not harm you.

This book provides content related to mental health and relationships. As such, your use of this book implies your acceptance of this disclaimer.

Mastering

THE

PSYCHOLOGY

OF GOLF

WITH

EMOTIONAL

CORE

THERAPY

A Simple and Effective Method
to Empower the Golfer's Mind

BY ROBERT MOYLAN

ACKNOWLEDGEMENTS

I would like to thank my daughter, Anna, who brings me great joy. I also want to thank Aimee and Hollister Schneider, who both are passionate about life and inspire me to do my best. I also want to thank all my clients who have worked hard in their therapy sessions. A special thanks to my editor, Mike Valentino. His patience and expertise were invaluable during the writing of this book.

CHAPTER ONE
An Overview of the ECT Process to Help Golfers

The goal of this book is to reach anyone who desires to learn how to be the best golfer they can be on the golf course and the best human being they can be off the golf course. When you master the psychology of golf you will maximize your performance both on and off the golf course. When you learn the ECT process for golf, you can easily transfer the techniques to any relationship stress in your life, giving you more energy and vitality both in your game and in your life. One of the best ways to do this is to get the most out of your golf game by letting go of the debilitating feelings of fear, anger, and grief that inhibit or cripple your golf game.

Emotional Core Therapy is the simplest and most effective behavioral psychology treatment available worldwide for most relationship stress including golf psychology, sports psychology, addictions, depression, anxiety, anger, personality disorders, childhood emotional trauma, and marital therapy. How does one test the validity of a sports psychology or self help book? What you have to do is list the top 10 to 20 stressful events in your golf game. With the 8 step ECT Flowchart in my book you can process most any golf shot or relationship stress that occurs in life.

It is really quite that simple. All you have to do is reflect on the 10 to 20 most stressful events in your golf game. Then write those events down on a sheet of paper. Once you have read Mastering the Psychology of Golf Using Emotional Core Therapy (the process sinks in through repetition best) you can then process your 10 to 20 stressful events through the ECT Flowchart. You will then have verified proof that ECT is the only behavioral psychology approach that is so simple you can use it for almost any relationship stress either in your golf game or in your life. No other psychology approach, religious teaching, or educational process can claim these results.

Up till now, the vast majority of sports psychologists, counselors, social workers, psychologists, psychiatrists, and golf gurus have been relying on psychology techniques/approaches such as Rational Emotive Therapy/REBT, Cognitive Behavioral Therapy/CBT, Dialectical Behavior Therapy/DBT, Acceptance and Commitment Therapy/ACT, Psychoanalysis, Motivational Interviewing, 12 Steps, even religious teachings such as Buddhism and Christianity to help golfers both on and off the golf course.

ECT uses some of the same teachings as all of the above approaches (along with my own unique research and findings) but has condensed the process to 8 steps. With ECT, there is renewed hope that golfers throughout the world and at all levels can be treated for their various stressful issues more effectively.

How can one prove the effectiveness of a psychology approach for golfers both on and off the course? Can we measure a psychology approach like we do with a major league pitcher throwing a fastball, or an Olympic runner racing in a hundred-yard dash? Unfortunately, we cannot measure any psychology approach, including ECT, over an extended period of time such as six months or longer. Too many variables exist that would adversely affect an accurate measurement. For example, not all golf psychologists have the same training. Educational and ability levels of golfers vary greatly also. Resources and environments can differ from one golfer to the next. There is something unique about how each of them experiences golfing and their life outside of the game. Also, each golfer carries new stress both on and off the course that would impact any study. When you try and assess psychology approaches measuring stress outside of golf you run into the same type of measurement problems. Far too many variables exist to get an accurate measurement.

Again, the only effective way to truly measure any psychology approach, including golf psychology, is to list ten to twenty stressful events that a golfer faces, both on and off the course. Then try and process them through whatever psychology approach you currently use. Then do the same with my eight step ECT Flowchart. There will be your proof! Only ECT effectively treats the root cause of a golfer's stress both on and off the golf course. ECT accomplishes this because there exists a cause and effect relationship with stress. The ECT Flowchart depicts how the natural state of stress occurs. For every relationship stress a golfer faces, both on and off the course, one thing happens with certainty every time. What is that? One of the four true feelings, joy, grief, fear, or relief will arise and occur. These four temporary feelings cause stress to golfers both on and off the course by altering a golfer's central nervous system.

You can't deny, suppress, or ignore the four true feelings for very long either while playing golf or in other aspects of your life. They will happen no matter what you do. Drugs and alcohol can only alter or dampen your five senses and four feelings. That's why golfers are some of the most stable professional athletes in sports. For the most part, they realize that taking drugs or medications won't change the conditions you face both on and off the course. Oftentimes, in fact, altering your mind/ numbing yourself up with depressants and stimulants will hurt your golf game and your life outside of golf.

ECT is one of the most important discoveries in the history of the field of psychology and mental health. Why? With ECT we have discovered the root cause of relationship stress! (This being the temporary arousal of the four true feelings.) With the eight step ECT Flowchart, we now have a psychology approach that can effectively treat the root cause of relationship stress for golfers both on and off the course. While not playing, golfers suffer the same types of relationship stress that all human beings face. The good news is that ECT is the simplest and most effective psychology approach to treat nearly all of the psychological disorders and relationship stress that people face. (The exceptions are some cases where permanent physical or psychological damage has occurred). Even activities such as throwing out your back lifting a heavy object or changing your golf swing can be understood clearer using the ECT Flowchart.

I've never encountered a stressful human interaction that I wasn't able to comprehend using the eight step ECT Flowchart. In some rare occasions it is hard to distinguish the exact variable that caused you stress. For example, hitting out of deep rough on a downhill slope on a cold windy day. You miss-hit the shot badly. Often, there are too many variables to accurately know what caused your stress of missing the golf shot. What you can always recognize is the true and authentic feeling of grief that follows. Very similar to a hungover college fraternity man who drank vodka, beer, smoked a joint of marijuana, and stayed up all night. He is not exactly sure what caused the pain...but he sure knows what he is feeling when he finally experiences the pain/grief.

Every golf shot a golfer makes, and every stressful event in his or her life (for example, divorce, financial loss, spousal abuse or neglect, parenting stress, backaches, swing change problems, gambling addiction) can all be traced back to the four feelings. Why not honor and learn from these four feelings? Why run away from them or disconnect from them? That is the focus of ECT. When you learn from your emotions you become more aware of what comfort level and limitations your body and mind have regarding the four emotions.

Think of it this way. Two gold miners are on a sandy beach hunting for precious metals. One miner has a metal detector that detects hundreds of metals, many of them useless. The other miner has a metal detector that can detect the four true minerals of value (for example, gold, silver, platinum, and aluminum). Who has the simpler and more effective method of mining? Obviously, the second gold miner. The same goes with emotions. We will show in this book that there are hundreds of names for emotions. When you can reduce the number down to the four true emotions, a golfer and golf psychologist will have a much easier job learning from them. Why? The four true and authentic emotions serve as a navigation tool or compass both on and off the golf course by helping you choose healthy relationships that bring you joy and leaving unhealthy relationships that bring you grief and fear. All my golfers and clients that leave therapy successfully have real power and confidence in their lives! Why? They leave therapy knowing they can have a relaxed, meditative state of being, very close to what is termed "mindfulness" in psychology circles. Then when any type of stress occurs in their lives, whether on or off the course, they have full confidence in the eight step ECT Flowchart, that they can identify, process, and release this situational stress and get back to a normal relaxed state of being. No other psychological, religious, or educational approach can do this as they are continually redirecting you away from your true emotional state.

Another example I use is a schoolteacher outside on the playground. One teacher has to supervise 150 children. Another teacher has to supervise four children. Who has the easier job? Obviously, the schoolteacher who supervises four children has the less stressful job. We breakdown needs in our ECT Flowchart into four categories also. The needs and demands both on and off the course are what cause stress to golfers. So when we simplify the needs and emotions for golfers both on and off the course we can help them learn more quickly and effectively.

Stress, in the form of the four true and authentic feelings comes shot by shot and hole by hole for golfers as they play. Off the golf course, they also face these four emotions hourly and daily. The key point for all healthy golfers is to learn to cathartically release these emotions. ECT is the most inclusive psychology approach worldwide as it can incorporate any psychological technique that is proven to help release emotions. I give over 20 examples in my books on how to successfully release emotions. Golf psychologists will learn to love ECT as many of the techniques they have learned in school (Eye Movement Desensitization Reprocessing/ EMDR, biofeedback, hypnosis, art therapy, etc) can be incorporated into ECT when problems off the course get serious. Even common ways of relaxing such as yoga, Pilates, sitting in a jacuzzi, listening to music on headphones, etc., can be easily incorporated into the eight step ECT Flowchart. Of course, psychology techniques we use for golfers while playing are much simpler as the emotions are not too serious. The key concept to understand here is portability or deliverability. What can the golf psychologist easily teach and deliver to the golfer that he can easily digest and learn both on and off the course? The goal is autonomy and independence for the golfer.

ECT is now being used throughout many parts of the world. Since joining LinkedIn last year, I have now been endorsed by thousands of professionals worldwide. ECT was the top rated book in two categories (Emotions and Mental Health) on Amazon in 2014. Approximately ten thousand people have read and reviewed ECT without any major criticisms of the ECT process! Why? It works every time to identify and release stress if used correctly.

Currently, I teach ECT to medical and mental health professionals both online and in person for continuing education units (CEUS) for their license renewal. This includes psychologists, social workers, counselors, nurses, marriage and family therapists, physical therapists, chiropractors, massage therapists, and several others. A dozen United States licensing boards have approved ECT for continuing education credit and renewal.

Golfers are keenly sensitive people. Professional golfers on tour have to be able to hit very powerful golf shots with their driver that go upwards of 280 yards. They also have to be able to delicately hit shots out of a sand bunker, or thick rough grass, with poise and a calm demeanor. This can only occur if they have control over their central nervous system and can block out loud noises and stresses like cheering crowds.

ECT is for almost everyone, regardless of age, race, gender, religion, or sexual orientation. Even non-readers can learn ECT if they have someone teach them the process.

This book will primarily focus on golfers, both on and off the course. For a book for teens that covers many of the common relationship stresses that young people face in their daily lives like job, school, family, and friend stress, see my book for teens, Emotional Core Therapy for Adolescents. For adults, my book, Emotional Core Therapy covers many of life's common stressors. Both of these books cover situational long-term stress like death, marital discord, divorce, job loss, etc. The techniques you learn in all three books will likely cover the vast majority of the stress that one endures as a human. Why? Nearly all of the serious stress that people face is situational and can be properly treated with the correct treatment plan.

We will discuss some longer-term situational stress in this book. Why? It is impossible to turn off your true emotions once you leave the golf course. Look at how off the course problems have hurt two major champions. Tiger Woods with his marital problems. John Daly with his alcohol and gambling issues. Both these major champions were adversely affected by off the course situational stress. Other longer-term stress like swing changes (Luke Donald and

Tiger Woods) and injuries (Steve Stricker) are also quite common for golfers.

I have a strong commitment to better the world and make it a more peaceful place. The psychology field can unite us as golfers and human beings if we work together and educate them to learn to really love themselves and love others. My hope is to have all mental health providers utilize ECT and bring people throughout the world closer together as human beings. I also hope that other religious, educational and psychological leaders can embrace ECT and help bring people closer together through a shared understanding of best practices.

Remember that knowledge is power! You and your fellow golfers all have been hurt and in pain from emotional stress of some kind both on and off the golf course. It is only human nature to be a bit "stressed out" from time to time. With ECT you will now have the tools to help yourself and others. ECT is the closest thing I know to an "Emotional Fountain of Youth". When you learn to cleanse your soul, one golf shot at a time and in your daily life, you can keep yourself feeling youthful all your life.

The goal of this book is to make you feel optimistic before and after each golf shot you take on the course. ECT shows you how to do this effectively. This book teaches you a simple step by step approach that will bring you closer to mastering the psychology of golf. The ECT Flowchart that you see on the adjacent page will be placed throughout the book at the end of each chapter. This will be beneficial for those visual learners who want to monitor their growth and progress in order to measure how much you have learned about the ECT process. A simple suggestion would be to use a highlighter or black marker at the end of each chapter to note which sections of the ECT Flowchart you are able to comprehend. The author does not want to cause the reader undue stress so he emphasizes that oftentimes we do some of the ECT steps automatically or instinctively.

A great way to learn sports psychology techniques is through storytelling. This book will utilize that approach as it makes learning the process of Emotional Core Therapy even simpler and more enjoyable. For readers who learn through a more interactive style, there will be a list of important concepts at the end of each chapter.

:

EMOTIONAL CORE THERAPY AND THE SCIENTIFIC METHOD

As you begin the journey to understand the Emotional Core Therapy process please keep in mind the scientific method. The scientific method is a process for creating models of the natural world that can be verified experimentally. The scientific method requires making observations, recording data, and analyzing data in a form that can be duplicated by other scientists. The subject of a scientific experiment has to be observable and reproducible. Observations may be made with the unaided eye or any other apparatus suitable for detecting the desired phenomenon. The apparatus for making a scientific observation has to be made on well known scientific principles. The Scientific method requires that theories be testable. If a theory cannot be tested, it cannot be a scientific theory. The scientific method requires and relies on direct evidence. This means evidence that can be directly observed and tested. Scientific experiments are designed to be repeated by other scientists and to demonstrate unequivocally the point they are trying to prove by controlling all the factors that could influence the results.

Source (Scientificpsychic.com/Scientific Method)

Here are the four steps to the scientific method and the Emotional Core Therapy process.

1). Observation made both visually and with scientific equipment

Stress occurs on the mind and body. There exists a cause and effect relationship with stress.

Often times this stress can be uncomfortable for humans.

2) Formulation of a hypothesis to explain the phenomenon in the form of a causal mechanism/method/approach.

Many psychology methods (REBT, CBT, ACT, DBT, etc.), religious approaches (Buddhism, 12 steps, etc.), and educational programs (Smart Recovery) have attempted to fully and completely explain via a model, how this cause and effect relationship with stress occurs. Up until this point in time, we have not had a model in the world that can successfully depict how this stress occurs each and every time. To their credit, many of these methods partially work and have contributed greatly to humanity. See Wiki.com for information on all the psychology methods and techniques mentioned in this book. With the invention/discovery of Emotional Core Therapy (ECT) we now have a psychology method that accurately can depict this causal relationship between stress and humans through Mr.

Moylan's Eight Step Emotional Core Therapy Flowchart. Complete explanations of each of the eight steps of the ECT Flowchart exist in the accompanying book. With ECT, we now have a psychology approach that identifies and treats the root cause of psychic stress. The root cause of psychic stress is the temporary arousal of one of the four true emotions (joy, grief, fear, and relief). ECT also shares and borrows many psychological techniques from the aforementioned approaches.

3) Test the hypothesis.

The Eight Step flowchart has been tested thousands of times by Mr. Moylan in many venues including his clinical practice as well as in his role of training other professionals. The ECT process works accurately to depict the situational stress affecting humans. Anytime someone experiences psychological stress, aspects of each of the eight steps of the Emotional Core Therapy Flowchart will be utilized and affected. Why does this phenomenon happen when one experiences stress? The Emotional

Core Therapy process highlights and identifies the key components of the root cause of stress. Anyone can test the model which is utilized extensively in this book.

4) Establish a theory based on repeated verification of the results.

Billions of people suffering relationship stress can be helped by Emotional Core Therapy. This includes stress on and off the golf course. Every effort needs to be made to ensure people suffering from stress have access to this model and accompanying treatment program in this book. Every effort needs to be made to educate the human population on the ECT process as all humans suffer stress from time to time. Because of the inclusiveness of Emotional Core Therapy, many effective psychology techniques that have been demonstrated to release stress can be incorporated into ECT. It takes time and will to learn and apply ECT. Behavioral psychology, including ECT has some limitations, which are addressed in Mr. Moylan's work. Some of the requirements to effectively learn ECT are a level of cognition generally at or above a high school level. Also, those with long term physical or psychological damage may not be able to utilize all steps effectively.

One of the most powerful benefits of ECT is its ability to incorporate any psychology or religious method that can successfully release emotions. The following approaches are some of the many techniques that have been shown to successfully release emotions. Gestalt Therapy, role playing, psychodrama, art therapy, music therapy, hypnosis, EMDR, biofeedback, Reiki, pet therapy, journaling, Mindfulness, some aspects of prayer, yoga, verbalization of emotions, etc, as part of the eight step process. View Wiki.com for detailed explanations of these techniques. Humans release stress in many ways and it is important to work from a person's worldview and utilize techniques that may be familiar to them.

The ECT process works just like entering data into a computer. You enter your own situational stress into the Emotional Core Therapy

Model to relieve stress and get back to a peaceful centered sense of well being. Relationship stress generally varies from person to person which is step one of the ECT Model. Generally, each individual experiences the four true feelings differently which is step six of the ECT model. People release their stress in a variety of ways which is step seven of the ECT model. And finally, everyone meditates/relaxes in a variety of ways which is step eight step eight of the process. Because of the many varied ways human beings experience and release stress, the ECT model and accompanying book will offer readers a user friendly approach to treating stress on and off the golf course.

ECT Flow Chart

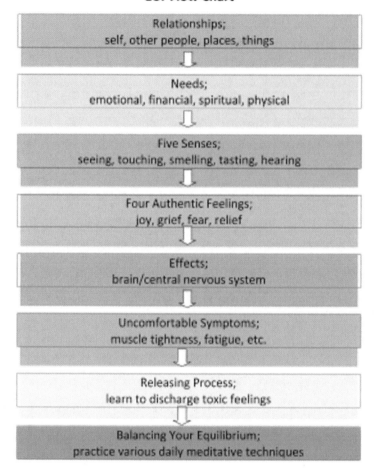

Relationships;
self, other people, places, things

⇩

Needs;
emotional, financial, spiritual, physical

⇩

Five Senses;
seeing, touching, smelling, tasting, hearing

⇩

Four Authentic Feelings;
joy, grief, fear, relief

⇩

Effects;
brain/central nervous system

⇩

Uncomfortable Symptoms;
muscle tightness, fatigue, etc.

⇩

Releasing Process;
learn to discharge toxic feelings

⇩

Balancing Your Equilibrium;
practice various daily meditative techniques

All golfers suffer stress from time to time. However, we're all individuals and we have plenty of differences, so how can a golf psychology book help such unique human beings? By concentrating on key principles, because what you'll learn here applies to all golfers. Every single one of us, at one point or another in our life will struggle with our golf game. There's absolutely nothing wrong with that. In fact, it's a perfectly normal part of being an athlete. What happens, though, is that as a golfer you often don't know how to handle difficulties in your game when they inevitably darken your doorstep. This is where Emotional Core Therapy (ECT) can help you. I've been practicing it and using it to heal golfers and other athletes throughout my career. Even better, you can learn how to use it to help yourself.

My approach to golf psychology and therapy is to first make sure that people realize that an anguished mind is every bit as painful (sometimes more so) than a hurting body. Of course, people feel compelled to seek medical assistance to set a broken leg or treat a sore throat. Yet, when it comes to our golf game and sports we are either embarrassed to admit that we have a problem, or confused about our treatment options.

It doesn't have to be that way. What's important is recognizing not only that you need help, but that you deserve it. Why would you deprive yourself of something that could be so beneficial to both your golf game and your life?

ECT introduces a group of techniques that are simple to do, and they work over time. More importantly, it empowers golfers to help themselves. If I could teach someone the perfect golf swing, but they can only do it when I am right there standing next to them, what good would that do for them? By the same token, what good is golf psychology and therapy if it doesn't work when you leave the therapist's office? That is a basic premise that I always keep in mind when teaching golfers about the power that all of us have within ourselves to release our pain and to feel better. ECT has a primary goal of autonomy for the golfer.

Emotional Core Therapy helps put structure and better performance on one's golf game by providing a simple framework. This new therapy approach examines the root cause of all emotional problems, which is entering and leaving relationships with people, places, or things. Once one feels the emotional pain of fear and loss, they start to examine their body and mind sensations. By learning to monitor their feelings, people can find out what has "hurt" them both on and off the course, and only then can they begin to fix their game. Consider the following phrases:

"Once bitten, twice shy."

"Fool me once, shame on you. Fool me twice, shame on me."

"The definition of insanity is doing the same thing over and over again and expecting different results."

Each one of these offers advice for identifying what it is that hurts us, along with a corresponding solution that implies we grow and learn from the conflict. This is the same fundamental logic of ECT, to learn from each time that we have debilitating feelings of fear and loss. Let's look at something as simple as putting on a jacket on a cold and blustery day. Most every child knows that to protect them from the cold, one has to put on layers of clothes to keep warm. It is something we all learn at a young age. This is the same dynamic we are doing with our feelings. Harmful feelings of fear and loss can cause harm and danger to one's body in much the same way that a snowy and wintry day can adversely affect a person dressed only in a T-shirt and shorts. ECT is a form of self-care that has as a desired effect the reduction of toxic pain. The goal of this book is to make the reader so familiar with the process that they can use it anytime, just like one uses a winter jacket. At the heart of Emotional Core Therapy is learning how to identify and process the four authentic feelings that arise from all relationships in golf and in life. They are joy, grief, fear, and relief.

Could it get any more human than that? It's for all of us, regardless of gender, race, sexual preference, economic status or religion. ECT is an approach that encompasses the entire human family. It offers a practical, realistic and very effective method for dealing with all of the stresses that a golfer faces both on and off the course. It all begins with you as a golfer honoring your five senses: hearing, seeing, smelling, tasting and touching. Pay close attention to all five of them. What are they telling you? You will never really know if you impair your senses with toxins such as caffeine, drugs, or alcohol. An individual who honors his senses will be more aware not only of the outside world, but of their own inner world as well.

I like to use metaphors. They've been invaluable in forming my understanding of the world in assisting those who come to me for help. I will use them throughout this book. A golfer needs to be honest with himself, and decide if their emotions on the course are helping or hurting them. For example, would an aspiring pro golfer who throws his clubs when he misses a drive, be an improved golfer if he handled his emotions properly? Can the proper understanding of emotions lower your score? How many shots does one throw away because of poorly handled emotions? Mastering the psychology of the mind is essential for any amateur or professional golfer who strives to be his best. The idea is to truly be comfortable with yourself as well as to learn to identify feelings that are uncomfortable. Let me explain. Consider a golfer that hits four to five excellent shots in a row. To the naked eye, no problem, he is playing well, so he will want to keep the positive vibrations going. Right? Wrong, that is not what the elite golfers do! If they do, they will elevate their central nervous system, and before you know it they will make an errant shot from too much adrenaline. That is why, to the contrary, elite golfers have a calmness about them. Most have learned to maintain a good, balanced psyche. It is also important to realize that it is possible to have too many feelings of joy and relief.

For an example outside of golf, think about an adolescent listening to rock and roll music. Some teens will rock and roll for hours. They get a mindset that life is more pleasurable than it really is. That sets up an unrealistic expectation to have, i.e., that life is always that pleasurable. In reality, though, one way or another, the party will be over one day. Some kids try and use substances to keep the elevated feelings longer. The point is, you can now begin to see how having too much of the authentic feeling of "joy" can also be problematic. Why? Because joy is a temporary state of being that elevates the central nervous system. If you get too excited it can adversely affect your golf game.

This emphasis on learning how to process our true feelings and properly handle our emotions not only goes well beyond golf, it actually applies to virtually all of life. Think about it, even without a major crisis, on a day in, day out basis we all have minor psychic pain of one sort or another. It could be a difficult to live with mate, a boss with a short fuse, kids who are always "pushing your buttons," etc. Though not debilitating, these daily irritants can build up and steal away your happiness and peace of mind. As you become more aware of your feelings, you will be better able to decide what you can handle and what you cannot. It may need to involve terminating certain relationships. For example, if a boss is so overbearing that you are living in misery, the only solution might be to find a new job. But there are also other techniques that can be used for identifying and releasing feelings, as we will see.

To help explain the many benefits of Emotional Core Therapy I want for you to imagine a rudderless rowboat rowing down the river. What does it take for a rowboat to traverse down the waterway? Fuel of course. In this case, fuel would consist of a healthy diet. By that we mean not using stimulants such as coffee, caffeinated soda, and excess sugar, all of which affect the central nervous system. All stimulants or depressants affect the four authentic feelings of joy, grief, fear, and relief. Minor uses such as a cup of coffee in the morning or salt on your popcorn, likely would not affect a person's central nervous system in a chronic manner. The best advice I can give here is to speak with your family doctor or nutritionist if you have concerns with your dietary intake. The important factor to remember is that food and drink can have a positive or negative impact on your central nervous system and may adversely affect your golf game. Although the topic of food intake is beyond the scope of this book, just keep in mind that the relationship exists.

Back to our rudderless rowboat...it's gliding through the water effortlessly and smoothly. Try and visualize the peaceful state of the rowboat as it courses downstream. Soft, tranquil, yet very sturdy. Quite a vessel, wouldn't you say? Now imagine if this rudderless rowboat was able to traverse the sea and ocean for months and years in the same manner. What an enjoyable experience. This is ideally, the emotional state of a golfer or person who has successfully learned ECT. Even if someone has never read a word about ECT, they could have this same feeling. How? By just staying emotionally balanced and healthy their whole lives. Sounds like a fun and enjoyable way of life. So what is so hard about achieving this state? Rather than give you the answer, let's realistically explore in this book what happens to golfers as they experience life using the rudderless rowboat example.

Now, with our rowboat traveling the waterways, what happens from time to time? Inclement weather affects our sturdy little vessel. High winds and rain, along with cold and hot weather seriously call into question the reliability of the boat to keep out water. From time to time, a big wave (rainstorm) causes water to leak into the rowboat. Consequently, the rowboat slows down and its power is weakened. If a tornado or hurricane passes in the path of the rowboat, you can be slowed to a near stop. This is in effect, what happens to golfers when their golf game and the relationships they are in go sour. Their vitality and passion for both golf and life becomes diminished when negative and toxic emotions adversely affect their central nervous system. Recall how it feels when you lose a close friend who you bonded with for several years, or any other human tragedy. The sadness that a golfer faces is similar to what has happened to someone aboard this fictionalized boat. When you are playing golf, the fears and sadness are obviously less than the long-term stresses in "real life". However, we still have to pay attention to the core emotions because they are always with us every hour of every day and we need to learn from them.

Taking the analogy a step further, we could reasonably ask why not just use the rowboat in a small river and have an enjoyable boating experience for life? The problem is, that is not generally how elite golfers operate. First of all, professional golfers and all athletes need food, water, and shelter to live. This takes money and resources to provide these invaluable necessities. Work has built in stresses like bosses as well as physical and emotional demands. Work requires training. This means schooling and education, which are all mandatory requirements of our youth. All of these demands will inevitably cause stress on the body and mind. Most of us (once again imagining the rowboat) will have water leak in from time to time. This book will teach you how to not have this stress negatively affect your game.

Another dynamic of sports and human nature is the needs and demands of golfers. Most, if not all of them will test themselves somewhat with wanting more out of their golf game; using the rowboat analogy, they prefer not remaining in the small waterway. Golfers will usually challenge themselves in competition to achieve as much success as they can. Whether it's golf shots or any other aspect of their game, gofers invariably find a way to partake in more and more relationships. As Emotional Core Therapy explains, it is the entering and leaving of relationships that can cause tension and stress in our golf game.

This book will teach you how to deal with your life both on and off the golf course. Examine the two lists below of commonly occurring stressful events in the game of golf and in life in general that can cause debilitating feelings of fear and loss. Here are some specifically involving golf:

1. Any injury that can adversely impact your swing. Muscle strains and sprains, especially those on key joints like knees, shoulders, back and neck.
2. Consistent lack of sleep or uneven sleep patterns.
3. Excessive anxiety playing in competition or with friends/peers.
4. High costs of playing golf including daily fees, golf clubs, golf apparel, and coaching.
5. Demands on time for playing golf rounds and practice time.
6. High demands that golf courses have for golfers. Sand bunkers, deep roughs off fairways, hitting over water, creeks, etc. Long holes requiring strength and power.
7. Difficult weather conditions that golfers face such as excessive heat, rain, cold, high winds.
8. Demands on the body to be properly warmed up, fully alert, and ready for each golf shot one has to make on the course.

9. Playing on time and within the rules. Typical golf game requires completion in four and a half hours.
10. Wear and tear on the muscles and body from competition.

The following list includes events that may come to you from your life outside of golf:

1. Death of a family member including spouse/child/sibling/etc.
2. Divorce or separation of a spouse.
3. Major health problem such as cancer, diabetes, etc.
4. Being fired or placed on review at work.
5. Problems or disputes with relatives or close friends.
6. Pregnancy or gaining stepchildren.
7. Being bullied at school.
8. Failing grades at school.
9. Marital affair/catching your partner cheating.
10. Being relocated at work.

Any one of the above stressful events can cause any golfer to suffer. The real difference is that emotionally healthy people, including those practicing ECT, appropriately process their feelings. There are literally hundreds of various relationship stresses that can possibly negatively impact a golfer while playing. Far too many to list and explain in a book. Once you learn the ECT process you now have a tool that can help you when you feel any stress on the golf course. I can't emphasize enough how learning to have a relaxed mindset both on and off the course will dramatically improve your game and your life.

The predominant state of a golfer that successfully has learned ECT is one of tranquility and a balanced equilibrium. The temporary feelings of joy, grief, fear, or relief do not dominate an emotionally healthy golfer. These four authentic feelings are just temporary states that affect the golfer from time to time. Let's face it. A perfectly smooth running rowboat does not exist for a golfer. It is not realistic. What is realistic is that one can expect some minor water coming in from time to time. In rare instances, a rushing torrent of flooding water threatens to sink the rowboat. A perfect analogy for when we need to learn and apply ECT or see a golf psychologist or therapist.

Let me describe for you what life would look like for an emotionally healthy golfer practicing ECT. This golfer is committed to a life of having peace and comfort on and off the links. Their mind is allowed to daydream and reflect. Reflection is key as it is a relaxed way the mind can roam and wander from thought to thought in an effortless manner. There is no effort underway to learn and acquire information. Cognition is another word for learning. That takes effort and taxes the mind. The beautiful state of meditation is different in that the mind is not charged with working on any stressful thoughts. I will show you how to learn this meditative lifestyle off the golf course first, and then we will apply it on the golf course.

One way off the golf course that we may be able to attain a healthy meditative state would be taking a bubble bath in a dimly lit room with candles and soft music. This atmosphere allows the mind to wander. A bubble bath is not possible for everyone on a daily basis of course, but the point is nonetheless well taken. One needs to create an atmosphere of self-soothing. There is just no substitute for taking time to relax every day. It is a way of loving yourself to allow oneself time to be rested and peaceful. When you can relax you have a great opportunity to let your mind wander and daydream. Oftentimes I work with clients for a month or two just on learning the valuable state of meditation. Here is a list of 10 popular ways to relax off the golf course:

1. Exercise before work, get the blood flowing.
2. Practice yoga, Pilates, or chi gong.
3. Do some gardening in the yard.
4. Escape by reading a relaxing book.
5. Get a neck or a foot massage.
6. Ride a bike in nature.
7. Journal, draw or paint your random thoughts.
8. Pick up a hobby you have neglected.
9. Plan a future getaway you would love to take.

10. Go out to a nice restaurant for dinner.

Ways to Relax on the Golf Course:

1. Slow, deep breaths.
2. Engaging in small talk with playing partner or caddie.
3. Appreciating and being aware of the beautiful landscape surrounding you. Trees, water, flowers, sand bunkers, etc.
4. Enjoying the walking and exercise on the course.
5. Singing to yourself. Using headphones and listening to music prior to playing.
6. Feeling the wind and being aware of the wind's direction.
7. Telling jokes or stories with playing partner or caddie.
8. Enjoying the smooth ride and glide of a golf cart.
9. Light stretching throughout the game to keep you fresh.
10. Embracing the adventure and fun of trying to improve yourself and your golf game.

I cannot emphasize enough how much a relaxed lifestyle will improve your life both on and off the golf course. The principle reason why is because it slows your central nervous system down and then you can identify and release stressful emotions easier.

So much of a golfer's pain can be avoided with proper care of one's emotional health. That is why I think it is so important for golfers to learn the techniques of Emotional Core Therapy, which is the primary purpose of this book. It is a way to take care of one's self in a preventive manner. Think about all of the other self-care techniques that you employ every day. Taking a shower and brushing your teeth for example. Both of these daily habits help keep disease away. ECT is also a daily habit, that when used correctly can help maintain one's emotional health both on and off the golf course. Even better, it is so simple that normal everyday golfers can practice the technique.

One of the most important benefits of Emotional Core Therapy is that you begin to examine why particular shots on the golf course cause you debilitating feelings. This enables you to learn from your golf shots and relationships and make better "relationship choices" next time. You begin to empower yourself by identifying and participating in better golf shot selection and healthy relationships, which in turn leads to more hope for the future.

In order to understand ECT one has to be ready to love oneself and protect oneself. It is also necessary to be willing to take a risk and practice something that you have not done before. This book about Emotional Core Therapy is meant as a teaching tool. That is why we used the approach of storytelling. It is a great way to teach as you can learn through others' experience in a joyful, non-threatening manner.

The alternative, simply ignoring our emotional needs or seeking relief in unhealthy ways, can prove disastrous. Oftentimes people begin to learn inappropriate self-soothing techniques and bad habits in their teens. My hope is that by writing in a short, storytelling, easy to read style, even young people can start to learn to process their feelings in a safe and healthy manner.

When we examine the escalating prevalence of mental health issues, we may ask the following question: is there a single remedy or psychological approach that works? If so, why don't we use it? Why don't we have a cure for mental health like we have for polio? The truth is we have a multiplicity of approaches that may alleviate many symptoms, but there does not exist one single approach that every therapist has utilized and every client has used and become healthy. There does not exist a one-size-fits all approach to therapy. If there did, all therapists would be trained in that approach and use it with their clients.

A similar question can be asked regarding ECT's simplistic approach. Why would ECT not help golfers to prepare for competition? What would be problematic when one processes authentic feelings? What happens when a golfer monitors their body for symptoms of stress and then works to alleviate those symptoms through commonly used psychological techniques? What could be problematic with the continued use of meditation and relaxation on a daily basis? What would be problematic about examining all relationships from a framework of entering and leaving them as a cause of stress? Well, the fact of the matter is that time and will (motivation) are needed for this approach to fully work. Why? Mature relationships, golf, school, friend, etc, frequently require the needs of others to be met. Even our own needs often have to be met in relationships. Whether it's emotional, financial, spiritual, or physical, humans are often required or asked to meet the needs of others in relationships. A key point of ECT is the concept of working to meet the needs of yourself as well as others in relationships. Golf puts tremendous physical demands on players while they are on the golf course, which is something that we will explore further later on in the book.

As we begin to discuss the benefits of ECT for golfers we need to point out that some may have to work longer and harder to reap these benefits. There are certain players who have impairments with one or more of their five senses (seeing, touching, smelling, tasting, and hearing). These impairments can cause their feelings of joy, grief, fear, and relief to be adversely affected. For example, a slightly visually impaired golfer may not receive the same response watching a movie at the theatre as a non-visually impaired person. Also, there are individuals who have suffered severe early childhood trauma that is permanent in nature. For example, a child suffering from fetal alcohol syndrome may have some sensory problems that affect the ability to sense and feel. It is not that some of the benefits of Emotional Core Therapy will not be utilized, but the desired outcome of learning ECT may be harder than usual. Another example would be those individuals in chronic pain. I have seen several patients over the years suffer debilitating accidents that cause acute pain. When the pain is so pervasive as to affect a person's entire day, they might not be able to fully sense their feelings.

What other situations would arise that would cause ECT to not be successful? This book outlines situations and exceptions where ECT may not have success. Like all treatment approaches people have to be comfortable with the process. Having the book told in a "simple storytelling fashion" is a means that has been successful with other psychological techniques, and I hope and trust that you will find it very helpful here as well.

If your goal is to be an excellent golfer and an authentic human being, then what would be more authentic than practicing ECT on a daily basis? What would be more authentic than respecting one's four authentic feelings? We have all heard of the book, "The Seven Habits of Highly Effective People." The book has a core premise that highly effective people all share certain key virtues, which may very well be true. Let's take this same framework for emotional health. What would the seven habits of an emotionally healthy golfer or person look like? I believe that it would be a great habit if you were to always honor your four true feelings both on and off the golf course. Meditation is a way of caring for oneself, so that is another great habit, as is honoring the four true feelings of others. In fact, as far as emotional health is concerned, those three habits would be a great way to live. So we might even jokingly refer to ECT as, "the three habits of emotionally healthy and highly effective people."

So if you're ready to finally love yourself to the core, to love yourself enough to care for yourself emotionally in ways that will improve your life forever, keep reading. You're in for a journey that will transform the quality of your being.

ECT Flow Chart

Relationships;
self, other people, places, things

⇩

Needs;
emotional, financial, spiritual, physical

⇩

Five Senses;
seeing, touching, smelling, tasting, hearing

⇩

Four Authentic Feelings;
joy, grief, fear, relief

⇩

Effects;
brain/central nervous system

⇩

Uncomfortable Symptoms;
muscle tightness, fatigue, etc.

⇩

Releasing Process;
learn to discharge toxic feelings

⇩

Balancing Your Equilibrium;
practice various daily meditative techniques

CHAPTER TWO
How ECT Works to Help Golfers

They say that "money makes the world go round," but that's not true. Emotions do. As a matter of fact, you could easily come to the conclusion that having emotions (also called "feelings") is what distinguishes us as human beings. What's most remarkable, however, is the range of emotions. There are well over 100. I've listed below a partial list of feelings to show the varied names we use for expressing ourselves:

1. Loving
2. Wonderful
3. Joyous
4. Happy

5. Peaceful
6. Satisfied
7. Ecstatic
8. Content
9. Serene
10. Pleased
11. Elated
12. Excited
13. Overjoyed
14. Glad
15. Festive
16. Thrilled
17. Enthusiastic
18. Eager
19. Cheerful
20. Optimistic
21. Anxious
22. Fearful
23. Tormented
24. Nervous
25. Pessimistic
26. Depressed
27. Helpless
28. Disappointed
29. Upset

30. Bitter
31. Frustrated
32. Inflamed
33. Incensed
34. Tense
35. Irritated
36. Skeptical
37. Unsure
38. Rejected
39. Offended
40. Heartbroken

These emotions can literally make us ecstatically happy or depressed to the point of utter despair. It has no doubt been this way for all of human history, but today modern psychology has unlocked the secrets of how we process our emotions. Learning how to do so in healthy ways, rather than harmful, is at the heart of Emotional Core Therapy. What ECT demonstrates is that no matter how many different names you have for these hundreds of different feelings, they all can be broken down, or categorized into one of four authentic feelings. These are joy, grief, fear, or relief. In this book, we will discuss both on and off the golf course stress. Why? Psychology techniques are learned behavior. Stress can be debilitating both on and off the course, so we always have to be aware of our emotional state of being. It is important for golfers to embrace a winning strategy in golf and life. Most golfers know the phrase, "Use it or lose it!" This phrase is used to remind golfers that if they don't continually practice their golf swing, they will forget their successful technique. Repetition and muscle memory are the hallmarks of every successful golf swing. Being aware of your emotional well being is a similar process. When you continually are aware of your emotional state, you own the process. If you try and ignore the emotions around you, you lose your awareness and knowledge of the mental process.

Think about it this way. Nearly all golfers want the power of a Bubba Watson driver. Bubba routinely hits the ball three hundred yards or further with his drives. That is impressive just like Michael Jordan making a dunk in basketball or Serena Williams hitting a powerful serve in tennis. We all love power. Off the golf course we all admire the power of people who live a life of passion and energy like your favorite movie stars. So the question needs to be asked. If ECT can help you have optimum power on and off the course, would you use it? Obviously yes! Hitting excellent golf shots is a wonderful experience. Living an excellent and wonderful lifestyle can be even better. In other words, why would you want to deny your true feelings (either on or off the golf course) when you know it will help you to live a more empowered life.

As you read this book you will come to understand that there is no single psychological technique that works for all golfers. That is because every individual is uniquely different and every mental health professional varies in their approach to therapy. As a matter of fact, I borrow heavily from a number of techniques from various schools of therapy to help my clients grow. For example, when I deal with addiction issues as the primary problem, I may try three or four different techniques from three to four different schools of therapy. I am not beholden to just one approach. The focus is always on the client's growth. So for an alcohol problem I may borrow techniques from several approaches:

1. Family Systems Therapy, which explores patterns from one's family of origin.
2. Cognitive Behavioral Therapy, which can sometimes focus on rewards and consequences to change behavior.
3. Gestalt Therapy, which uses role playing to help clients to see outside of themselves.

We won't go into detail on these other techniques. I only mention them here to make it clear that there are a plethora of legitimate and effective approaches for dealing with emotional issues for golfers. Keep in mind that in graduate school, therapists are trained in specific specialties, and I'm not here to advocate one approach over the other or to denigrate or critique others' work. As a golfer, you will of course have to discover for yourself what will work best in your own life. What I do want to emphasize is that, within the multifaceted mental health world, ECT utilizes fundamentally sound psychology techniques to treat a variety of common emotional ailments within a simple and effective framework.

Today, golfers are becoming more and more aware of the critical role that stress plays when it comes to both our mental and physical well being. Incredibly, we now know that stress is the number one killer of the human species. An overburdened psyche (filled with excessive fear) or a depressed psyche are not healthy for anyone long term. You simply cannot tax the central nervous system for too long without ramifications.

Yes, the link between stress and heart disease and all kinds of other diseases is well established. But the overriding question is what can we do about it? Forget the idea of completely eliminating stress from your golf game. That's impossible. Each new day brings with it the possibility of stressful situations. It simply comes with the territory when living in an imperfect world. There are always going to be things that we find stressful. Playing golf involves experiencing all four of what, as you have learned, are termed the "four authentic feelings." These are joy, grief, fear and relief. My main focus in counseling golfers/athletes and other clients is to have them understand these four authentic feelings. Anger is a reaction to grief and is also analyzed in counseling sessions. All four affect your golf swing.

In simple terms all four true or authentic feelings evolve from entering and leaving relationships. Let's take a look at the following diagram. As you can see from this diagram, when you go towards something you like there is "joy". What is joy? In simple terms, it is a pleasurable state of arousal. Most people can understand this sensation if you ask them the question, "What are you most optimistic about?" Their answer will likely be directed towards a relationship they are happy about entering into. An example would be seeing your favorite sports team win a close game, or maybe smacking a drive right down the middle of the fairway. Another example would be hugging a loved one or someone you admire.

Flow Chart of Four Primary Feelings

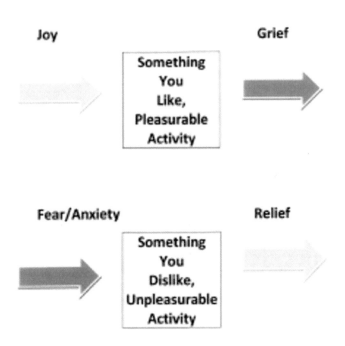

Joy

Grief

Something
You
Like,
Pleasurable
Activity

Fear/Anxiety

Relief

Something
You
Dislike,
Unpleasurable
Activity

Grief is what happens when you leave a relationship that you enjoyed. An example might be hitting a golf ball into the water and taking a penalty stroke. Or perhaps leaving a loved one when you go off to work in the morning.

This diagram also shows what happens when you enter a relationship that you dislike. A relationship that you dislike will provoke feelings of fear. An example would be climbing inside a cage with a hungry lion. For golf, it might be hitting out the back of a sand bunker on a downhill slope.

When you leave a situation you dislike, there is relief. For example, escaping out of a cage in which a hungry lion had been running after you. Or maybe hitting the ball into the trees and finding out that you still have a reasonable chance of reaching the green.

This flowchart of the four authentic feelings is critical to understanding Emotional Core Therapy. Please go ahead and test the validity of the four authentic feelings by substituting several of your own stressful experiences both on and off the golf course for those that we have listed here. Try several for each authentic feeling and you will see that the flowchart is an accurate depiction of what happens to us golfers throughout the day when we are playing. Stress, in the form of fear and grief will be with us our entire lives. ECT is the only therapy approach that addresses this stress openly, honestly, and accurately.

To see how the full sequence of events occurs with Emotional Core Therapy, let us now look at another diagram. This time we will examine the eight logical sequences of events that occur when authentic feelings are aroused and released. This diagram takes us from beginning to end in the ECT process.

As the ECT Flowchart below highlights, it is relationships that cause the four authentic feelings of ECT to arise. Specifically, relationships with our selves or others usually involve needs being met. For the sake of simplicity, I organize needs into four categories. Emotional, financial, spiritual, and physical. On the course, stress comes from relationships with the golf course, our clubs, and competition to name a few. Therefore, we have to be vigilant about the demands that we face. On the course, our five senses – hearing, touching, smelling, tasting, and seeing – are needed to help identify the four authentic feelings that arise when we enter or leave a relationship. These four authentic feelings send messages to the brain, which is part of the central nervous system. Oftentimes when one of the four authentic feelings are severe or debilitating, our body will feel uncomfortable with symptoms of stress such as muscle tightness, shaking, or fatigue. This stress can adversely affect our golf game.

The benefit of ECT is that it simplifies the identifying of feelings thus allowing golfers to be empowered with their emotional being. With ECT, we are recognizing that all relationships require needs to be met. Sometimes these needs are emotional, sometimes spiritual, sometimes financial and sometimes physical. It is a lifetime challenge to learn how to meet the needs of ourselves and of others.

ECT teaches a golfer to cathartically release these feelings in an appropriate way. Furthermore, ECT works with golfers to learn and acquire a calm, meditative state of being that is free from stress. This technique allows future authentic feelings to be more easily identified and processed. I would suggest that you review the ECT Flowchart and examine the eight concepts that demonstrate the ECT process from beginning to end. After studying the ECT Flowchart several times, try and envision a particularly traumatic golf shot or event in your life. Did your experience resemble the sequence highlighted in the ECT Flowchart? If so, how did your experience mirror that of ECT? If not, do not worry. We have the entire book to help you learn the ECT process. Remember, ECT can be easily transitioned to help with any sport such as basketball, tennis, football, etc.

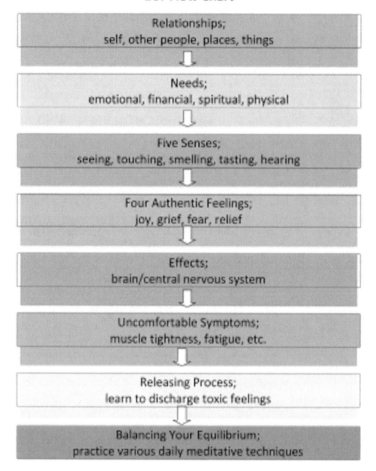

ECT Flow Chart

Relationships;
self, other people, places, things

Needs;
emotional, financial, spiritual, physical

Five Senses;
seeing, touching, smelling, tasting, hearing

Four Authentic Feelings;
joy, grief, fear, relief

Effects;
brain/central nervous system

Uncomfortable Symptoms;
muscle tightness, fatigue, etc.

Releasing Process;
learn to discharge toxic feelings

Balancing Your Equilibrium;
practice various daily meditative techniques

When you enter a relationship that you like there is joy (this is not limited to relationships with other people, as it could be many things; think of eating your favorite ice cream). When you leave something that you like there is grief (saying good-bye to someone you love). When you go towards something you dislike there is fear. Imagine walking near a snake pit. When you leave a fearful event, there is relief. Ask any golfer and they will tell you that playing golf is in itself a relationship – a relationship with nature. The tougher the golf course, the tougher the test is emotionally on a golfer's psyche.

Grief (otherwise known as loss) and fear (otherwise known as anxiety) are the two most debilitating feelings that golfers face when they play. Unfortunately, for most amateurs every round of golf is filled with these unwanted feelings. Golfers of every level need to get a handle on their emotions each time they play, or face the consequences.

Hopefully, this is all starting to make sense to you. Yet, you very well might be asking, "Well, that's great for problems on the golf course, but what about everything else in life?" My answer: ECT does indeed pertain to every area of our life. We all need to find healthy ways to process our emotions every single day, wherever we are and whatever we are doing. It doesn't matter how old you are, your financial circumstances, your love life or anything else. Your emotions are always there. They are an integral part of who you are. It makes no sense to try to bury them or to ignore them. Even if you could, you wouldn't want to, as it would be a shallow existence to live in a world without feelings. Some people try, through drugs, alcohol and countless other means. They often fail and end up harming themselves even more. That's precisely why it is so vital to learn how to best cope with toxic/debilitating feelings. Think of ECT as a lifestyle choice that will improve your mental health both on and off the golf course.

Like any lifestyle change, what you learn through ECT will not take root overnight, but over the course of months or years. It has to become integrated into your life and your golf game. Most emotionally healthy people do various stages of Emotional Core Therapy without much thought given to the process. However, for ECT to be of true value throughout one's life, it is imperative to learn the process completely. The goal is to never forget the process of how emotions work. We spend a year in high school learning Algebra, which many of us forget a few years later. That's OK if we go on to careers that never require Algebra. But we will always have emotions! So why not learn a process of emotional healing that will serve us our entire lives no matter where we live or what we do?

All of us humans know our dates of birth, our race, ethnicity, religion, etc. Why? We know these facts about ourselves because we learned them over and over again when we were young. We also were required to know these facts about ourselves at various times in our adult lives. It takes time and energy to learn these important pieces of information about our life. This information is useful and necessary as it serves to ground and center us as human beings.

ECT is also an approach that will allow you to be centered both in your golf game and in life. We will cover in this book many of the stressful events that golfers frequently have to face. As ECT explains, grief and fear are an inevitable part of life. In any given year it is likely that one in five people will incur a debilitating experience emotionally. Why not equip yourself for something so common in life? That is why we have placed an ECT Flowchart at the beginning of the book and at the end of each chapter as a reference point. This allows you to gauge how much you have learned about ECT after reading a chapter. A checkpoint of key ECT issues lets you focus on key concepts at a leisurely pace.

Remember to be kind to yourself and allow yourself ample time to read the entire book. It takes time to reflect on your own experiences as well those of others. If you were going to teach a child the ABC song, how would you do it? Would you be compassionate? Supportive? Would you give treats and rewards to the child when they learn portions of the song? Why not do the same for yourself when you learn ECT? Why not be kind and supportive and reward yourself for learning something as important as protecting your own mind?

The crucial point to remember is that the process of learning ECT is easier than it looks.

In fact, many of us use some of the various steps of ECT without even knowing it! For example, most people use their five senses hundreds of times a day. Most people are bombarded by other's needs (emotional, financial, spiritual, physical) throughout the day. Also, most people have messages or information sent to their central nervous system throughout the day.

Remember, the ECT Flowchart highlights eight concepts that typically occur in a relationship to cause us duress. The real work of this book is to understand five or six major concepts (understanding relationships and their needs, authentic feelings, mind and body distress, releasing feelings, and dutiful meditation). Two other concepts (understanding the five senses, and the central nervous system being affected) occur quite quickly and without much thinking. This book will only touch briefly on the two remaining parts of the ECT Flowchart that occur rapidly to all golfers on a daily basis.

Part of the overall ECT process we do instinctively anyway! For example, we enter and leave relationships all day long. So this is really not all that difficult for us to understand and follow. If you allow yourself the time to learn ECT, and are willing to commit the process to memory, be prepared to enjoy greater vitality and vigor. You are learning a process that will increase your enthusiasm and appreciation for life.

In order for ECT to be of real value, you need to be able to incorporate the contents of this book into your day to day life. This can only occur when the ECT technique is learned and committed to one's long-term memory, which only happens through repetitious work. In other words, practice, practice, practice. Over time you will enter the various steps into your short-term memory. After repeated use, ECT will eventually become lodged into one's long-term memory. Take a look at the diagram below to see visually how your memory works. We continually input information into our short-term memory until it is fully learned or acquired. When something like a golf swing is fully learned, it is stored in your long-term memory.

How Memory Works

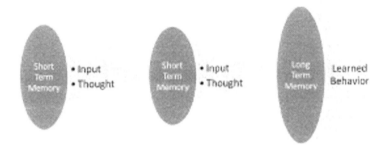

Once a person has the technique in their long-term memory, the process is learned and available for use. If you still have trouble understanding how memory works, think of remembering a ten digit phone number. Usually it takes several tries to learn a long phone number. The ECT process requires that one monitor his mind and body for feelings and muscle response. This effort takes time to learn correctly. As you become aware of all four feelings, and their effect on you, rest assured that you will start to become more emotionally balanced. You will learn how to apply this process to both your golf game and your everyday life. In this book I will be using practical examples and cases where ECT can and would be utilized. By processing the various scenarios facing everyday common folks, you will begin to commit the approach to your long-term memory.

To help you understand ECT, let's examine how the four feelings are processed. It is our senses – seeing, touching, smelling, tasting, and hearing – that process of all of our feelings. When a golfer can sense fear (such as hitting your ball over a daunting water obstacle) a message is sent to the brain, which is part of the central nervous system. The central nervous system in turn transmits messages to the muscles throughout the body. This same dynamic happens throughout the day to all of us in various degrees whenever we sense fear.

As a therapist, my theoretical orientation is described as technically eclectic. This means I use a variety of psychological techniques from a variety of schools of therapy. Over the years I have found that focusing on the release of authentic feelings has been helpful for my client's growth and development. Much like getting caught in a thunderstorm, the vast majority of golfers can become overwhelmed by emotions and lunge for the nearest umbrella. ECT, when practiced effectively, can downgrade a severe thunderstorm to just some minor drizzle. Emotional Core Therapy is effective because it filters out ambiguous words and negative thoughts by emphasizing and understanding the four true and authentic feelings.

It all begins with learning to continually monitor the four feelings. We all embark on the process at a different point in life. In my years of using ECT, I've had golfers who have come to me at various stages of growth. This approach offers hope for those golfers who have suffered even the most stressful events both on and off the golf course. Some are very emotionally healthy and need just a few sessions to get back on track. Others may need help in only one or two areas of life. I have empathy and compassion for all of them regardless of the stage of life they are in. This approach offers hope even for those who have suffered the worst possible cases of trauma and abuse.

Stressful events, as most every golfer unfortunately knows, come in a wide variety of shapes and sizes. The good news is that ECT is a helpful treatment option because of its inherent ability to authentically assess your problems in a simple, yet effective manner.

The goal of Emotional Core Therapy is to get golfers to be as peaceful and emotionally centered as a healthy two-year-old. The definition of having a peaceful, relaxing, and meditative state is to feel non-threatened, or affected, by the four authentic feelings. In other words, to have a relaxed and calm central nervous system. Envision an infant in a crib, smiling and relaxed. Just as an infant can sit in a crib in a blissful state, a golfer can also achieve a calm and relaxed state of being. As you read this book you will learn techniques to achieve meditation throughout your game. Meditation, a calm state of being, is essential for golfers desiring to use Emotional Core Therapy. Once you learn and can comfortably practice a calm, relaxed, sense of self, it becomes easier to identify the four authentic feelings.

Most golfers suffering from grief or fear (which, as we said, is also known as anxiety) come to my office in a sad state of affairs with little hope of feeling better. One technique I use is to have them reflect on a peaceful state of mind that they had sometime as a child. It may have been at school, on a beach, with a friend, etc. I then help the golfer realize that he can get back to that proper state of mind through utilizing many of my therapy techniques. This book will cover many of the most effective psychology techniques known to release feelings.

Of course, none of this is to imply that we're dealing with childish problems, or even trying to trace the problems back to childhood. Instead, Emotional Core Therapy teaches techniques to help yourself to learn how to process emotions properly, and in ways that are healthy rather than destructive. Remember that the four authentic feelings ultimately all stem from either entering or leaving relationships. Take, for example, a golfer and his wife who are having a strained relationship. Basically, their problem is "working on the marriage." Marriage is a lot of work, as each partner has to learn about the other partner's needs. In marriage counseling, I often make a list of what the husband and wife need emotionally, financially, physically, and spiritually. Both have to grow and learn about each other. With Emotional Core Therapy, we pay attention to how each feels in the relationship. The wife (Sally) in this scenario tells the therapist, "I get scared when John comes home from work. I know John works hard at his golf pro job during the day. His working conditions are not ideal as he has to deal with all the inclement weather and a mean and demanding boss! Still, I cringe when he comes through the door in his foul moods every day."

With ECT, we focus on the meaning of her feelings. In this case, both words she uses, "scared" and "cringe" are different vocabulary names for the authentic feeling, "fear".

What Sally is saying is that this relationship she has entered into brings fear into her life from time to time. The wife is not saying she has a terrible marriage. She just wants to address her relationship with her husband and work towards a better resolution in this particular situation.

With Emotional Core Therapy, there is a primary belief that no one deserves to live life with unwanted and toxic feelings. Furthermore, ECT has at its core a belief that withheld or internalized feelings are harmful for anyone in the long term. ECT utilizes a wide variety of commonly known techniques to release feelings. One of the most common techniques out there is to "verbalize" one's feelings. By talking out your fears with a compassionate golf psychologist or therapist, toxic feelings such as fear (otherwise known as anxiety) are released. This is called catharsis. Catharsis is the cleansing of the soul. With ECT, we are vigilant about cleansing our soul. Just like a young child learns to brush their teeth and wash their hands as a daily habit, your soul also needs this type of positive treatment.

There are other ways that Sally can learn to cleanse her soul. She can journal, listen to music, exercise, meditate, etc. Throughout the book you will find examples of releasing techniques.

If the wife comes in with lots of complaints of fear/anxiety because she is afraid to confront her husband for not listening to her, I may focus on her learning to be more assertive with her needs. In this example, the first step is identifying the fear.

This is similar to a golfer who says that he has a panic attack every time he has to hit out of a sand bunker. He has excess fear, which adversely affects his central nervous system, and in turn this change in temperament adversely affects his golf swing. Why? The golf swing needs to be free of tension and smooth to be effective. It needs to be able to be repeated over and over in a calm manner. When a golfer lets his feelings have a negative effect on his swing it is called "choking". In other words, his nerves get in his way. A golfer will utilize a swing coach and perhaps a golf psychologist to help him through his emotional problem. Both the swing coach and golf psychologist will be supportive, caring, and allow an environment for the golfer to take risks, and to make changes with his swing. If the golfer feels excessive fear in part of his game, he needs to trust his coach to get him better. Do you see how this is similar to a woman suffering fear from her husband? That's precisely why, when I use Emotional Core Therapy I encourage clients to take risks and make changes if they are suffering debilitating feelings of fear and loss.

Another example might involve an angry amateur golfer who is the father of two young boys and who works a lot. He comes to therapy to get some parenting skills. He tells me, "I am overwhelmed by these two boys and hate that I sometimes yell or get angry at them." Clearly, he chose his words carefully. The young father used the word "overwhelmed" because the reality is that he has too much fear! He's fearful (worried, concerned...feel free to add your own) that he will "fail" to fully or adequately complete all of the many tasks and responsibilities expected of him based on his circumstances and position in life. The solution, then, is that he needs to be organized and structured in such a way so that he can feel a sense of accomplishment with these necessary parenting tasks.

All of us adults can relate to this father as we all get overwhelmed from time to time. The dictionary definition of "overwhelming" is overpowering in effect or strength. Let's consider what is really happening to this young man in terms of the four authentic feelings. Without a doubt, he is moving towards someone or something he does not like. Let me be clear, I am not saying that he does not like his children. In fact, part of his fear is that, because he loves them so much, he's desperately afraid of failing them. He fears that he might not be up to the task, however, because it includes so many things that worry him. For example, he may love to ride bicycles with his two children. But then the two boys invite their two friends, meaning dad is now responsible for four kids. What then happens if they ride their bicycles near a busy street? The situation, he fears, could very easily spin out of control. What was once manageable and enjoyable, is now overwhelming.

Emotional Core Therapy will help this young father by isolating the problem, assessing the cause, and providing appropriate relief. We see that additional fear creeps into his thinking about this new activity as more children are involved, and in a more dangerous situation. When you have too much fear, it's important to reduce it somehow, if possible. A beneficial approach may be to highlight the new tasks and responsibilities involved in the four children scenario. By focusing on how the dad feels (muscle tension, lack of sleep, headaches, etc.) we can get him to modify his activities with his children. In the future, once the dad learns the technique, he can utilize ECT in other fearful, stress-inducing situations. Examples might be when he feels too much fear at work, or in other relationships. The point is, once you learn the techniques for processing your four authentic feelings, you will be amazed at how much this knowledge makes fundamental differences (for the better) in your everyday life and in the "big issues" (family, health, relationships, finances, etc). When I speak of "big issues" I mean "life events". Emotional Core Therapy has the ability, when used correctly, to alter one's outlook for the better, both on and off the links.

Earlier in this chapter we used the analogy of a thunderstorm versus drizzle to compare how one can feel less overwhelmed when using ECT. We utilize a similar framework for understanding life events. There exist hundreds, if not thousands of life events that can adversely affect the human psyche of golfers. On the course, injuries, tough competition or forgetting correct form with your swing may cause stress. Death, divorce, job loss, or financial loss are just a few problematic life events off the golf course. With Emotional Core Therapy we are compartmentalizing all of these life events into two categories: entering and leaving relationships. Emotional stress is caused by moving towards or away from a relationship you have with a person, place, or thing.

We are now ready to begin to explore the most commonly occurring emotional stresses in the life of every golfer. In the upcoming chapters we will examine hypothetical as well as actual cases where ECT can and has proven to be effective. As you read the various scenarios unfolding before your eyes, you can finally begin to learn the benefits of Emotional Core Therapy. In my work providing golf psychology, the most common psychological issues I see are depression, anxiety and anger issues. Most of these stresses to our equilibrium occur when we are playing golf or with family, friends, at work, school, or in a relationship with a partner such as marriage. I will examine how ECT can help golfers from all walks of life. As you become more and more acclimated to the ECT process, you will begin the healthy journey back home to yourself. Think of the movie, "The Wizard of Oz." The main character, Dorothy, relates to the "Good Witch of the North" at the end of the film, repeating over and over, "There is no place like home." This reassuring chant allows her to leave the fantasy world of Oz and return home to Kansas. This is the mantra that you need to learn to fully comprehend Emotional Core Therapy. Every golfer is lovable. Every golfer deserves peace. Every golfer can overcome their troubled emotional state.

Keep in mind that Emotional Core Therapy works if you allow the process to work. If you are willing to make a genuine effort to grow and develop as both a golfer and a human being, what you read in the following pages will be transformational in your life. Over time, ECT empowers the client by giving them the confidence that they can overcome many of the major traumatic events in life. There is simply no cure for the emotional trauma that life throws at us from time to time. From losing golf matches, to injuries, financial losses, and many other stresses, we are all tested from time to time. It is how we respond to these hurtful events that define us both on and off the golf course. ECT instills a therapy approach that strengthens the mind and helps protect the spirit of each golfer.

List Five Alternative Words Used To Describe The Feeling Of "Joy"

A) GLAD

B) HAPPY

1)

2)

3)

4)

5)

NOTES:

List Five Alternative Words To Describe The Feeling Of "Grief"

A) DEPRESSED

B) SAD

1)

2)

3)

4)

5)

NOTES:

List Five Alternative Words To Describe The Feeling Of "Fear"

A) ANXIETY

B) DREAD

1)

2)

3)

4)

5)

NOTES:

List Five Alternative Words Used To Describe The Feeling "Relief"

A) RELAXED

B) REPRIEVE

1)

2)

3)

4)

5)

NOTES:

List Five Stressful Relationships (Golf Shots, People, Places, Or Things) In Your Life

A) SWING CHANGE

B) FRIEND GETTING SICK OR INJURED

1)

2)

3)

4)

5)

NOTES:

List Five Ways You Can Relax In A Meditative State

A) SWIMMING

B) SOAKING IN A HOT TUB

1)

2)

3)

4)

5)

NOTES:

ECT Flow Chart

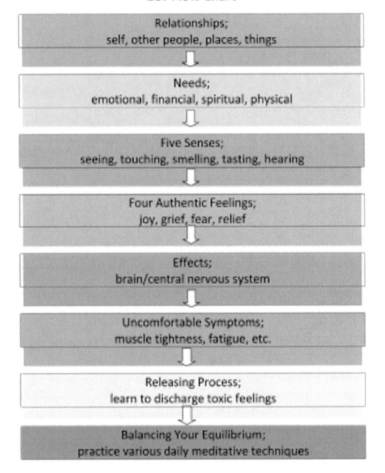

Relationships;
self, other people, places, things

Needs;
emotional, financial, spiritual, physical

Five Senses;
seeing, touching, smelling, tasting, hearing

Four Authentic Feelings;
joy, grief, fear, relief

Effects;
brain/central nervous system

Uncomfortable Symptoms;
muscle tightness, fatigue, etc.

Releasing Process;
learn to discharge toxic feelings

Balancing Your Equilibrium;
practice various daily meditative techniques

CHAPTER THREE
Helping Golfers with Grief and Loss

As we begin this chapter focusing on the authentic emotion grief I want to introduce a song that was originally a hit back in the 1960s. Entitled, "Love is All Around Me" it was remade in the 1990s by the Scottish rock band "Wet Wet Wet" for the hit movie, "Four Weddings and a Funeral". The song has a peaceful, calm and soothing backdrop and mirrors the kind of demeanor that a true golfer maintains both on and off the golf course. I would like to briefly describe the movie, as there are parallels to being a successful golfer.

The main characters in the movie, played by Hugh Grant and Andie MacDowell, meet and fall in love while attending four weddings and a funeral. The movie and song both have an easygoing nature and scenario as they highlight the passion of falling in love. Both the main characters are optimistic and upbeat as they repeatedly meet in chance encounters at four weddings and a funeral. The movie is filled with lots of ups and downs and awkward moments not unlike a round of golf.

I wish I were able to write a golf psychology book without discussing the feeling of grief. But just like in the movie mentioned above that is not realistic. Grief, like joy, is a part of every round of golf. The real key to being a successful golfer is how you respond to grief! Are you honest with your emotions both on and off the golf course? Can you allow yourself to learn from your four true emotions? Both the characters in the movie go to painstaking discomfort to be honest with themselves. They both realize, after repeated attempts to deny their love, that they are indeed truly in love.

There also goes the challenge to every golfer. Can you see the beauty of the game of golf? Can you also see the beauty of life? When you learn to master your emotions both on and off the course this becomes distinctly possible. Why? You slow your mind down enough to learn from each golf shot on the course. Likewise, when you're away from the game, you begin to learn from each relationship. This can only come from being fully aware of the four true emotions that are with us in every shot and every relationship we encounter. Just like the song, "Love is all around you", be kind and supportive of yourself while you are learning this invaluable tool to help your golf game.

I will begin showing you how to embrace the feeling of grief on the golf course by showing you step by step a few situations where golfers need to "own the feeling of grief" and learn how the eight step ECT process works. Before I do, I want to share one more instance of how a golfer experiences joy in their round in a step by step example. I believe that golfers, as with people in general, like upbeat and realistic books. After all, the movie was not a hit because it showed four funerals and a wedding and was primarily a sad movie. The movie was successful because it was filled with joy, fun, and optimistic scenes. Just like I hope every round of golf you play entails. Just like I hope every day of your life entails.

An example of joy affecting a golf shot can be seen with a golf pro named Tony. I was working with Tony and another pro named Tom on the golf course in a competitive practice round. Both players were tied going into the 18th and last hole. Both players were in the fairway on a short par four course. Both were only a 130 yards out with clear shots at the pin. Tom hit first and missed the flag, landing on the fringe about 50 feet from the hole. Tony came up to his ball very excited. He knew that if he put this ball close to the hole he would have a great chance of winning the match. His adrenaline was pumping and he felt extremely eager to hit his approach to the green. Tony quickly set up over the ball and struck it. Because of his excitement and adrenaline flow, Tony hit the ball too hard. His shot flew clear over the green into a hazard and he lost the match. Afterwards we talked about his shot. He agreed he was too excited (excess feeling of joy) and his central nervous system was elevated. With his elevated central nervous system, too much blood, oxygen, and water were flying through his muscles. Thus causing an errant shot. After the match, Tony wanted to learn how he let his emotions cause him to lose the match, so we went through the eight step ECT Flowchart that is at the end of each chapter in my book. As I mentioned to Tony, any stressful event on and off the golf course can be understood and processed with ECT. We just needed to have Tony learn and apply it to this situation where he lost his match. As I mentioned to Tony, there is a difference between losing and failure. Everyone loses from time to time. The difference with champion athletes is they learn from their emotions and mistakes while quitters don't learn. They just give up and keep making the same mistakes and failures over and over again.

Step one of the ECT Flowchart is understanding that entering and leaving relationships causes stress. Relationships take many forms, including the relationship we have with ourself, other people, places, or things. In the case of golf shots, we are primarily talking about the relationship one has with a golf course and golf club. So for Tony, the first step in understanding his emotional pain by mis-hitting his shot was understanding his relationship choice. In this particular case he chose a nine iron to fly the golf ball 130 yards. Normally, a nine iron would have been a great choice, except Tony was too pumped up for the shot.

The second step of the ECT Flowchart is understanding that each relationship we enter into requires needs to be met, just as every relationship in life. My ECT process simplifies these needs down into four categories. Emotional, financial, spiritual, and physical. An easy way to comprehend needs is to examine the relationship you have with your spouse or friend. Usually, we are meeting all four needs of others on a daily basis. I explained this to Tony this way. When you listen to your wife talk about her day, you are meeting her emotional needs. When you give her money for groceries, you are meeting her financial needs. When you give her a hug when she comes home from work, you are meeting her physical needs. When you go to church with her, you are meeting her spiritual needs.

In the particular case of Tony we are talking about a physical need that the golf course demanded from him. He was required to hit the ball into a mild wind from a 130 yards away. Without the demands of the wind, Tony would have used a pitching wedge. He weighed all the factors that would affect this shot correctly, except one, his emotional state of being.

The third step of the ECT Flowchart is that we perceive which needs are to be met through our five senses. These are seeing, touching, smelling, tasting, and hearing. For Tony, in this case, he utilized his sense of sight, touch and hearing all to properly measure the golf shot. Tony saw his yardage. He touched and grasped his golf clubs. He then checked the wind with his eyes and by feeling the wind with his ears and seeing the flag wavering. This step happens quite quickly for most of us both on and off the golf course.

Step Four is understanding which of the four authentic feelings were affected by this relationship. In this particular case, Tony was overly excited about winning the golf match. Excitement is just another word for the true emotion of joy. Tony's joy came from entering a relationship he liked. He felt excited to have the opportunity to hit his golf shot and win his match with his golf pro and friend Tom.

Step Five is emotions then get sent to your brain, which is part of your central nervous system. The central nervous system sends messages to your muscles and tendons. This step is pretty much automatic for all humans most of the time. This includes Tony for this particular shot.

Step Six is understanding what symptoms arise from the four true emotions. Generally, when we are dealing with toxic emotions we are identifying toxic emotions that feel uncomfortable. Although the feeling of joy is pleasurable, it is nevertheless an emotion that can alter the central (CNS) nervous system. Remember that when we alter the CNS, we alter the blood flow to our muscles, which can adversely affect the shot. Golfers want to limit blood flow and excess energy in their swing, as routine and consistency are needed for a fluid golf swing. In the case of Tony, the golf pro, he recognized, after the fact, that he had excessive joy in this particular case of the 130-yard golf shot.

Step Seven is the releasing process. Learning to discharge toxic emotions. A quiet and calm demeanor is essential for golfers, as they need to hit various shots that require strength and a soft touch. Since all four authentic feelings adversely affect the golf swing, we want to limit them as much as possible. THIS IS ONE OF THE MOST IMPORTANT KEYS TO GOLF. WE NEED TO IDENTIFY AND RELEASE THESE FOUR EMOTIONS EVERY TIME WE HIT A GOLF SHOT. If we can learn to do this after every swing of the golf club we are putting ourselves in position to get the most out of our golf swing and golf game. In the case of Tony, he recognized that he did not properly release his excess feeling of joy/excitement before his golf swing. He let his emotions hurt his swing. Tony and I discussed some of the ways he would have been able to release these emotions. In this case, we mentioned slow, deep breathing as a way to calm himself down. By learning this technique, Tony began to calm his central nervous system down. He was very open minded so we discussed using his breathing as a way to monitor his monitor his body both on and off the course. A real break-through occurred months later when Tony was able to learn to apply ECT throughout the day, again both on and off the course. Once Tony was able to get to that stage, his golf game and his quality of relationships improved. He felt more confident that any time he felt undue stress, he had the eight step ECT Flowchart readily avail-able to handle future stress, either involving golf or life in general.

The eighth step of the ECT Flowchart is to balance your equilibrium. To practice various daily meditative exercises. Tony's wife was a hot yoga enthusiast, so he decided to join her yoga class several times a week. He began to slow his life down both on and off the course. This proved invaluable for Tony as the more he became relaxed, the more he was able to identify and process the four true feelings which were hurting his golf game.

Once you learn ECT, you can usually go through these eight steps on the golf course in a matter of seconds or a minute or two. The actual learning of the ECT process usually takes from five to ten hours to watch my fifty minute video and read my book. The exercises in the book help you learn and apply ECT to your own life. This process of applying ECT to your life usually takes weeks and months. This can be seen and understood just like learning a particular golf swing. Once you take a lesson, you then have to try it out. No one gets it the first time, every time. There is usually some trial and error process taking place. Again, be nice to yourself and treat yourself well while learning ECT.

The next case I would like to share with you is about an amateur golfer who I worked with named Joe. A high handicapper, Joe frequently thought of quitting the game of golf. He described his golf game as a love/hate relationship. He enjoyed the nature and camaraderie of playing with friends but was very unhappy about how he played golf. When I spoke with him it became clear that he enjoyed golf a great deal but had trouble with several parts of his game. He frequently scored double bogies or worse with his game because he had a poor driver off the tee and a poor sand bunker game around the greens. We worked on both issues over several months and his game improved dramatically because Joe was able to learn from the mistakes he made on the golf course. Besides working with me as a mental coach, Joe was able to get a teaching pro to help him with his golf shots. It is important to have a swing coach who can quickly and effectively help golfers with their mechanics.

Joe and I worked on his shots that were causing him immense grief or sadness on the golf course. Sometimes when Joe would hit his driver off the tee box, he would slice the ball. This usually occurred with one out of every three or four of his swings of his driver. The ball would either end up in the trees, in water, or out of bounds as he had a way of really mis-hitting the ball where it would go fifty to seventy yards offline.

After Joe hit his driver he would go and look for his ball in a state of sadness. He knew that he would be scoring poorly on the hole and was worried his friends would laugh at him. He was also quite embarrassed that he would look so horrible sometimes. Joe oftentimes would not be able to regroup in time to hit his next shot. In other words, he kept his sadness long after the shot occurred and usually for a few holes. Joe and I discussed how ECT can help both him and his golf game if he learned to identify and process his emotions each time he hit the ball. This meant learning from his emotions, and not letting them spoil his round of golf.

Joe and I started out by examining one particular time he sliced his driver. This occurred at a golf outing at work. Joe did this four times during the round and felt horrible. This particular time he went home sad and stayed that way till he went to bed.

Joe and I examined this problem with his golf game using the eight step ECT Flowchart. The first step was understanding that each golf shot was a new and real relationship, separate from each other shot. Step One states that relationships with ourselves, other people, places, or things, cause us stress when we enter upon them. Joseph began to realize that his grip, his stance, and his position of his ball at address were causing him excessive grief from time to time.

In Step Two, Joe was understanding that each new relationship he entered into required needs to be met. As we mentioned in our earlier case with Tony, oftentimes the needs/demands on a golfer are physical. In this case, Joe had difficulty understanding how his body, stance and grip would make him hit such terrible shots.

Step Three of the ECT process for Joe was understating that his five senses are involved in processing the oftentimes-stressful needs/demands on the golf course. Joe learned that he was gathering his information though seeing and touching. This step happens quite rapidly and automatically for most people, including Joe.

Step Four was understanding which authentic feeling, joy, grief, fear, or relief was aroused when he sliced with his driver. In this case, the authentic feeling was grief. Grief feels uncomfortable for every golfer, including Joe. He realized he would not be able to play golf like this for much longer.

Step Five is when this feeling of grief gets sent to Joe's central nervous system. The brain is part of the central nervous system which sends messages to our muscular system. This step is very automatic for almost all people. In other words, it happens whether you like it or not.

Step Six is understanding the uncomfortable symptoms our body presents when we have one of the four true feelings. For Joe, he felt slight tension in his chest and a sinking feeling in his arms and shoulders. He began to lose hope and confidence after slicing the driver.

Step Seven is the releasing process. Learning to discharge toxic or debilitating emotions. For Joe, he tried several different techniques to release his emotions. He would verbalize his emotions to his friends in a silly manner. "Oh there goes that crazy slice!" "Where did that come from?" "I feel like a turd." This was a good start for Joe as he was externalizing his emotions versus holding them in. Stress comes with us shot by shot and hole by hole on the golf course. Joe was learning to cathartically release these emotions versus holding them in and feeling miserable.

Step Eight of ECT is to learn to balance your equilibrium and practice daily meditative exercises. Joe began to take his time in between each shot and enjoy his surroundings. Joe would look at the trees, water, and flowers that were part of his golf course. Joe took the time to appreciate this quite scenic beauty which is a part of most golf courses. Off the golf course, he began to take his dog for long walks and enjoy the scenery in the subdivision where he lived. Slowing down and relaxing is the hallmark of most all successful golfers. Having worked with many athletes across many sports, I often find that a relaxed mind is essential. Once ECT is truly learned, you can apply the process to any sport. Joe would go bowling during the winter months. He remarked how he was able to transfer what he learned on the golf course to the bowling alley. As I pointed out to Joe, the demands of a bowling alley are different than a golf course but the ECT Flowchart and the core emotions stay the same. Joy is joy, wherever you go. Ditto for the other authentic feelings. The intensity of emotions can vary depending on the relationship or sport you are involved in. Missing a golf shot or throwing a gutter ball will take a back seat to getting fired from a job or having your girlfriend/boyfriend break up with you. This aspect of ECT is critical for all golfers and people in general to grasp. The four feelings never change when you go from relationship to relationship. WHAT DOES CHANGE IS THE FREQUENCY, INTENSITY, AND DURATION OF THE FOUR FEELINGS. This is all the more reason to "own" the ECT process on and off the golf course. Familiarity of what is truly a part of all of us will make you a more powerful and independent person.

A final thought on the case of the amateur golfer Joe. A remedy would not come right away for Joe as he would have to try several real different techniques working with his teaching pro to fix his swing. Over the course of several weeks, Joe was able to get rid of his slice and learn a more effective swing. It is also important to note it took several months for Joe to master ECT. Just like reading this book, you can't learn ECT from just reading one chapter. It takes repetition to truly learn something of value. As we go case by case and story by story, the ECT process and Flowchart will sink in. Each chapter has interactive exercises at the end to help you become more aware of how you feel. There is also a test at the end of the book that will help you measure comprehension. The last exercise in the book has you list your own stressful golf shots and apply ECT to your own golf game. Hopefully by then, you will be a master of ECT. If for some reason you miss learning a particular step of ECT, you can always go back and reread the section you need to fully understand the process.

A third case I would like to mention in this chapter is the case of Emily. She was a competitive golfer who came to me suffering from grief or minor depression. In my assessment of Emily, I discovered that her grief/sadness was primarily caused by a nagging back injury. Emily had strained her back lifting her toddler son, Gavin, who was almost two years old. Emily was also a part time yoga instructor who worked three to four days a week. It became apparent to me that Emily was doing too much repetitive motion on her lower back causing inflammation from time to time. The flare ups in her back would happen at any time. They occurred when she was standing over a putt, teaching intricate yoga motions, making golf shots, or lifting up her toddler. Emily once had a beautiful golf swing that was one of the best among her peers. Now, with her back injury, she was not always able to finish her golf swing and started to miss shots. Emily tried to play though the swing but she kept on feeling a sharp twinge in her back. She had trouble getting in and out of the golf cart and walking the course made things worse.

In our weekly sessions I was able to help Emily understand her problems. Her excessive grief on and off the golf course was due to her back injury. Her attempts to play through her injury were making her injury and her grief worse. Why? The ligaments and tendons in your body can only endure so much. How much torque you can demand on your swing varies from person to person. When I work with my clients I always have them rate their pain from 1-10 with 10 being the worst pain possible. Emily often felt her physical pain was a 7-8. Her level of sadness would usually be around a 4-5. Without her back pain, Emily was very happy with her life and often would report her emotional state as a 1-2 and feeling very good about life.

I referred Emily to a local physical therapist who gave her exercises to do to strengthen her back. She also did some cardiovascular exercise on the treadmill to oxygenate her inflamed joints. Meanwhile, Emily stopped playing golf for a few months to decrease the inflammation in her back.

Emily began to regain strength in her back and learned better techniques to lift her toddler son. On the golf course, Emily learned to limit her practice swings and cut back on her days of playing golf from four times a week to twice a week till she fully healed. She also reduced her hours at work for a short time. Over the course of five months, Emily was able to get her back feeling better. She reported both her golf game and life back on track. She felt comfortable with making minor changes in her lifestyle to ensure her long-term health.

Let's again visit the ECT Flowchart to examine how ECT helped Emily. Remember, the ECT Flowchart can be used to understand any human relationship stress. Often times, when someone has multiple variables that cause them stress (for Emily, it was traumatizing her back muscles by excessively using them at work, home, and for golf). It can be a chore to identify exactly what caused you stress. More important however is to understand which authentic feeling is being aroused. In Emily's case the feeling was grief. As I explained to Emily, when you put your hand on a hot stove once, you won't do it again anytime soon! Why? You learn from the true emotion of grief. With ECT we learn to take responsibility for all our relationships both on and off the golf course. Only when we fully embrace our role in choosing relationships can we grow and learn from them. Emily was very willing to embrace ECT and became a better golfer and mother because of her willingness to learn how the mind and body work together.

Step One of ECT is recognizing that entering and leaving relationships is what causes one stress. This includes relationships with ourselves, other people, places, or things. For Emily, lifting a 20-pound toddler boy was a relationship she entered into that caused her stress.

Step Two is recognizing that the needs of relationships we are involved in are what cause us stress. Needs can be broken down into four categories for simplicity sakes. These are emotional, financial, physical, and spiritual. The emotional needs of the toddler, Gavin, prompted Emily to go and lift him in her arms. The lifting was a physical need that Emily perceived that the boy required.

Step Three of the ECT Flowchart was recognizing that the five senses (hearing, touching, smelling, tasting, and seeing) are how we perceive the stressful needs of others. For Emily, she listened to Gavin cry and saw his emotional pain. She used her sense of touching to lift the toddler boy up in the air. In her golf game, she would exacerbate this injury by taking a full swing with her driver and irons which would cause her grief/sadness.

Step Four of the ECT Flowchart was understanding that relationship stress evokes one of our four true (joy, grief, fear, or relief) and authentic feelings. In the case of Emily, her repetitive motion of swinging a golf club and straining her back caused her excessive grief.

Step Five of the ECT Flowchart is understanding that these authentic feelings cause stress to humans by altering the central nervous system. The central nervous system sends messages from our brain to our muscular system. This step for Emily, and all humans, happens quite automatically.

Step Six of the ECT Flowchart is understanding the bodily discomfort and uncomfortable symptoms that are presented with most of our stressful encounters. Although joy is a pleasurable human emotion, golfers need to learn to release this emotion as it can alter your golf swing. For Emily, she had fatigue, tiredness and a loss of energy after playing golf and with Gavin. Why? Emily was doing too much repetitive motion to one side of her body when golfing, which was exacerbating her physical pain. Ditto for lifting her toddler son. Golfers have to be aware of when and why physical pain is occurring and "own" the pain. By owning the pain you have, you can make the necessary changes to your lifestyle and begin the healing process.

Step Seven is understanding the "releasing process" that needs to take place. Hourly and daily stress can cause us bodily discomfort so we need to learn to release this stress hourly and daily. Emily would make a list of all the golf swings that caused her pain and grief immediately after each golf shot. By making mental notes of each swing and writing this down on paper, Emily was beginning to own and release her emotional pain.

Step Eight of the ECT Flowchart is to balance your equilibrium and practice daily meditative exercises. By quieting your mind and slowing down your lifestyle, you then have a much
greater opportunity to identify and process the
four true feelings, which are the root cause of
stress to golfers. Emily learned to listen to quiet
and relaxing spa music when she was at home.
When she was practicing golf she would listen to
her spa music on the driving range. She would
hum her music/sing to herself in between golf
shots when she was playing competitively.

Grief for golfers happens everywhere on
the golf course. Why? We enter into many different types of relationships on the golf course.
Sand bunkers, deep grass which makes hitting
the golf ball harder, long holes requiring strong
driving, steep sloping putting greens which
cause putts to change directions, are but a few of
the many ways we feel moments of sadness and
grief on the golf course. Sure, no one is going to
call an ambulance and head to the Emergency
Room over minor grief on the golf course. Yet
grief alters the CNS and can adversely affect

your game. More importantly, learning how to release this grief soon after a golf shot will ensure you have an optimal swing for your next golf shot. The key is habit formation. A golfer utilizing ECT is learning to cleanse his soul after each golf shot. This repetitious nature is needed when one is under stress from competition. Whether you are playing a practice round with your buddies or playing in the US Open, shot preparation remains the same. All you are thinking about is preparing for and executing the shot at hand. This necessitates cathartically releasing your emotions effectively after each swing. Every golfer needs to learn to have a "quiet mind" before hitting each golf shot. If a golfer ever starts to feel anxious and begins to think about external stress like crowds, competition, scores, etc, you have to regroup. Step back from your golf swing and focus on releasing your emotions until you get back to your peaceful and centered state of being.

Our four true and authentic emotions serve as navigation tools on the golf course by helping us identify shots that bring us joy and eliminating those that bring us fear and grief. It is vital for every serious golfer to take note of the shots when you are playing. Oftentimes we can't correct our swing when we are playing competitively. That's why, if we take written or mental notes of our golf game, we can head to the driving range or chipping/putting green and try and correct our swings.

Repetition is key for any golf swing as the more you can make your golf swing fluid and automatic the less chance stress will adversely affect your golf game. The same goes with your mental game. It simply won't work to just use ECT on the golf course and then disregard your emotional state off the golf course! Why? We continue to embark on relationship stress off the course in our daily lives. Off the course, the four true feelings are with us hourly and daily. If you choose to ignore these feelings you will regress in your emotional development. You will learn bad habits and coping mechanisms that you will inadvertently take back on the golf course.

As we transition our focus on ECT to present cases off the golf course where relationship stress has hurt golfers, let's keep one important aspect of ECT in focus. Learning and using ECT off the golf course can optimize your well being. A healthy relationship with ourself and others can only begin when one is emotionally healthy. A healthy or stable person, as seen through the lens of ECT, is a person who has full awareness of the four authentic feelings. Furthermore, a healthy person knows a relaxed and meditative lifestyle.

A healthy relationship is built on mutual respect. The communication style is one of openness and honesty. Lying and stealing are not part of a healthy relationship. Being able to trust and share one's authentic feelings is paramount to a healthy relationship. One can only do this if the relationship allows for a caring atmosphere where all feelings are welcome and understood. This means one has to be able to share feelings of fear and loss as well as joy and grief.

One of the important aspects of ECT is you begin to understand why particular relationships cause you debilitating feelings. This allows you to learn from your relationships and make better "relationship choices" next time. You begin to empower yourself by identifying and participating in healthy relationships, which in turn leads to more hope for the future.

Now we are ready to explore grief in deeper detail where it occurs off the golf course. Our focus turns to understanding how to identify and resolve grief off the golf course so that it does not become problematic while you are golfing. Again, I want to revisit a thought I had at the beginning of the book. Look at how off the course problems have hurt two recent major champions. Tiger Woods with his marital and injury problems. Also, John Daly with his alcohol and gambling issues. Both of these major champions were adversely affected by off the course situational stress. Other longer-term stress like swing changes (Luke Donald and Tiger Woods) and injuries (Steve Stricker) are quite common for golfers.

Emotional Core Therapy offers realistic, creative solutions for those who find it difficult to escape depression's grip. Consider what might be a "worst case" kind of depression scenario.

We all remember the catastrophic tsunami in Japan, and all of the misery that it brought to so many people. Imagine the case of a forty-year old woman in Japan. When the tsunami swept over her town, her husband died, she lost a child and her community was devastated. All of her money was lost. Now if ever there were cause for depression, this would be it. What could help this woman? Would she suffer for the rest of her life? How could she possibly recover?

I bring up an extreme example like this to challenge our thought processes. Why? The truth is, every month and every year people do survive and recover from tragedies such as this throughout the world. They even overcome these seemingly insurmountable troubles without the benefit of ECT or any other therapy for that matter. How do they do it? All it really takes is time and will for things to get better if one appropriately allows the normal occurrence of processing feelings to take place. With ECT, people are taught that all of us have the power to overcome any loss or devastation that life may throw at us. Yet, we also need to recognize that there are different levels of difficulty with whatever problems we may be facing (depression, anxiety, etc.) That is why it is important to try to rate the level of mental pain that a person is suffering. If we use a scale of one to ten, one would be when a person has virtually no problem at all, while at the opposite end of the spectrum ten would be when the problem seems almost unbearable. When there is an extremely serious problem, especially with something like depression, if it is a nine or ten that person may need to seek immediate help in a hospital Emergency Room or your nearest doctor. However, for more moderate ailments, say a four, five, six, seven or eight, an approach such as using Emotional Core Therapy can help treat the stress.

Time and therapy are an incredibly powerful combination. Of course, it requires trust on the part of the client, and both client and therapist must view themselves as partners in the therapy process. This in turn gives power to the client. How better to give power to the client than to have the client become their own therapist?

One of the most important things that we do is to identify the relationships that would benefit the client, like loved ones, friends, etc. What would be required to help them? For starters, often just being with a therapist helps, which is why the therapist needs to be accessible at various hours. Atmosphere makes a big difference too, so the office should have a kind and sincere ambience. It should also be remembered that grief does not always get resolved quickly. Trying to rush things would be counterproductive, which is why therapists always allow the unpacking of feelings to occur at its own pace.

There is, however, one big obstacle that too often gets in the way before the process can even begin. Golfers, like all human beings, have a propensity to spend countless hours and far too much energy running away from debilitating feelings of fear and grief. But they are running in the exact opposite direction. In ECT, the goal is not to avoid our feelings, but to learn from them. For example, a very talented teenager twists her ankle doing a back flip in gymnastics practice. She is so traumatized by the pain that she is shaken to the core with fear and decides to quit the gymnastics team. Think how much better off she would be if she analyzed her feelings rather than attempting to bury them. Instead of hanging up her shoes and ending her career, she could ask her coach, "How did I land improperly? What caused the injury? What can I do to prevent it from happening again?" If she had learned Emotional Core Therapy, she would have understood how to respect her authentic feelings of fear, and then release it by discovering how to improve her technique, rather than quitting the sport.

How can she do this (respect her authentic feelings)? By learning how to monitor her own body and the signals that it is constantly providing to her. That is a crucial facet of ECT, and it can in fact be transferred to all kinds of situations in life. The releasing of feelings can involve any loss in life, or any fearful event. Since we are all unique, none of us will release our feelings in the exact same way. It's a bit of a discovery process. For example, I had one client who had a maid who would come by to clean his house. He would then have long conversations with her. She had four kids, and she would tell him about her problems and how she dealt with them. Having five children of his own, this turned out to be something that they shared in common and just talking with this woman helped him to release his feelings.

A different client, in this case an ironworker, would release his feelings on the massage table while carrying on a conversation with his massage therapist. The point is, releasing feelings is a very natural process, and often takes place in unexpected places and usually unintentionally. It does not by any means always have to take place in a therapist's office.

Another example could involve a young, shy 19-year old male. He falls head over heels for a girl at his community college. Sadly, after three months of intense dating, she abruptly breaks up with him. Emotionally devastated, he withdraws into a shell and does not date for four years. Now ask yourself, would it have been much more emotionally healthy for this young man to instead honor his pain of grief/loss? I believe yes! Rather than stop dating women, he needs to accept the experience and view it as part of a learning process. Easy? No, not by a long shot. It takes time (often months and even years) to understand one's feelings, which is why it is a continual learning process to learn ECT. But the benefits are real and often life-changing, as in this case where the young man could start dating again within a year or so of his loss, rather than languishing in turmoil and unresolved grief for at least four years.

As these examples illustrate, we can learn a lot by examining various real life scenarios of golfers and individuals struggling with golf and the stresses of life, which is precisely the approach of the rest of this book. The goal is to help people learn how to cope effectively with debilitating feelings. Oftentimes I see clients have "breakthrough" moments in therapy when they realize they can control entering and leaving relationships. Clients feel empowered by seeing that the relationships they enter are of their own choosing. Furthermore, these relationships will invoke one of the four authentic feelings to occur. All my clients tell me they would rather experience the feelings of joy versus fear or grief. It is helpful for clients to then work towards joyful relationships. Let's go back to our analogy of a rowboat. Why would a rowboat owner choose rocky waters? Why would a person want fear and grief in their life? When I work with my clients to empower themselves to make healthy choices they become more confident.

Of course, the best way to learn something of value is to experience it ourselves. This is not always practical, not to mention desirable. For example, have someone go to the bank and withdraw all of their money. Then the person would take their life savings and burn it in an incinerator. Sure, that would most definitely cause tremendous grief and fear. We would then be able to demonstrate how processing the four authentic feelings of ECT would help the person suffering this financial loss. But since pursuing such a reckless path would be completely illogical, the next best thing is to share the success stories of people just like you and me who have very effectively used ECT to recover from emotional trauma. One of the primary purposes of this book is to demonstrate several psychological techniques in a fun and relaxed manner. It can be quite a comforting process when we identify with the experiences of others.

At its core, ECT involves externalizing one's feelings rather than internalizing them. There is a time and a place for cathartically releasing feelings, and common sense must be used. What we are trying to do is to get our feelings outside of us, and this is a process that takes time, like learning to ride a bike or to swim. For example, imagine if you lost $50,000 in some kind of financial scam. Do you think that you would just bounce back from something like that overnight? Of course not. The feelings of anger and loss would be all too genuine, and properly releasing them would not come quickly. On the other hand, however, it would be quite regrettable to put this off too long, which would be very unhealthy for both your mind and body. Toxic beliefs, if internalized, can cause unnecessary stress and damage to the body. This in turn leads to body function problems such as muscle tightness, hand sweating and trembling. Don't underestimate the seriousness of this. A person who is under stress all of the time is risking damage to their organs, which is of course extremely hazardous.

Let's look at the example of a local PGA teaching pro who came for therapy because she found that she was in a depressed state. In fact, this woman, Teresa (like all examples in this book, a fictionalized name is being used to protect this individual's identity and privacy) was suffering from minor depression feeling lethargic, having trouble sleeping, a lack of energy, and feeling hopeless at times. I approached her as I do all of my patients, with a goal of recovery. Over the course of fourteen years she raised her two children and worked full time as a golf pro teaching others the beautiful game of golf.

Unbeknownst to Teresa, her husband had an affair with a schoolteacher. Soon, he and Teresa began to live separate lives while under the same roof. For a time they briefly separated which caused stress for the two children.

When Teresa came to my office her level of depression was about a seven or eight on a scale of 1-10 with 10 being the worst possible depression. She was already under a psychiatric doctor's care for depression. Teresa came to me with complaints of being "lonely, sad, tired," and playing horrible golf! Once a three handicap golfer, Teresa was shooting 8-10 over par when she played. It was not difficult to assess her problem as too much grief or loss. This is another name for depression. Teresa also had several bodily symptoms including lack of sleep, trouble eating and feeling fatigued. In short, the hopelessness that she felt was so bad that it negatively affected her central nervous system.

Using Emotional Core Therapy we started to reframe some of her thinking. She began to recognize that most of her thoughts were due to leaving a long-term relationship. In this case, her husband of fourteen years. Her overwhelming feelings of psychic pain began to lessen over time as she learned to isolate the problem. As she became more and more aware of the four authentic feelings, she recognized that she had too much grief in her life. Over the course of three to four months, she began to release her feelings both in therapy, in her daily life, and on the golf course. Every client and golfer is unique. I often have to try several different techniques before we have success in releasing feelings of grief. In Teresa's case we had great success using psychology techniques that involved role playing. I would pretend to be the husband and we would reenact some of the situations that caused her emotional pain. By doing this in the non-threatening environment of the counseling office, Teresa was able to finally express herself properly. She was finally able to release her psychic pain. Another technique we used was to have Teresa talk to an empty chair. The empty chair was a non-threatening way for Teresa to get her anger (otherwise known as grief) out of her mind and body. Sometimes the pretend person in the chair was her husband. Sometimes we had Teresa talk to her "pretend self" using the empty chair technique. By having Teresa approach herself in a kind manner she began to have compassion and empathy for herself. Teresa learned to be kind to herself by using healthy and upbeat language to address to herself how she was feeling.

Another way that Teresa and I were able to combat her depression was by working to bring more joy into her life. We made a list of ten new ways she would make herself happy and joyful. As we discussed this list of ten joyful character-istics a main theme continued to pop up. She also started to do things that brought her joy herself. For example, she began to power walk for exercise and stress reduction. Teresa was able to reduce her level of depression from a seven or eight level to a two to four level over the course of our therapy, which utilized some ECT techniques.

One of the most effective ways to treat depres-sive symptoms both on and off the golf course is to have clients learn a meditative lifestyle. Teresa, like many of my clients was introduced to mindfulness. This is a method of keeping one-self in the present moment rather than letting fear and depressing thoughts pre-occupy your thinking. Mindfulness was an excellent fit with the approach and goals of ECT that Teresa was learning as the more she learned about ECT, the more she came to understand that such meditation could be an important addition to her toolbox of techniques that she was compiling for finally dealing properly with her depression issues.

During meditation, Teresa would sit in a comfortable chair and begin by concentrating only on her breathing, in and out slowly through her nostrils and feeling the gentle rise and fall of her abdomen. When her thoughts would begin to wander, she would merely return them to the simple act of breathing. This brought about the desired effect of bringing stillness and quietude to her mind. This helped Teresa to process her emotions in a much more healthy way, just as she was discovering by learning and using the ECT process. Mindfulness is a terrific way to relax and meditate on the golf course also.

Mindfulness is a highly effective technique to calm the central nervous system down. Over the years, I have seen golfers and regular clients make better decisions when they have a calmer state of being. That being said, Mindfulness is one of many excellent meditative exercises one can do to bring tranquility in their lives. ECT strives to work from a client's perspective so with each new client we research their history. We try to find what has worked in the past and what each client is comfortable in doing as a meditation exercise. As a reminder, a meditative lifestyle and state of being, is the eighth step of the ECT Flowchart. We may not always be able to achieve this goal on a day to day basis, but the more we make an effort to stay calm and relaxed and make mental health a priority in life, the better chance we have of identifying stress.

Teresa also cut back on drinking the two to three glasses of wine each day. Alcohol numbed Teresa's pain but did little to change her underlying condition of a poor relationship. She began to decrease her drinking as she saw it as a form of escape or addiction. Teresa worked hard in counseling and her overall emotional health improved both on and off the golf course. It is important to highlight cases such as Teresa because forces outside the golf course caused her stress yet her golf game suffered. Complete ownership of being a winning golfer means having a mastery of the mental game. In order to master the mind, one needs to apply ECT in all facets of one's life.

Many clients such as Teresa try to self-medicate, which can take myriad forms. Some like going to the casino and playing the slots, or maybe having a few beers. They are using these things as a way of trying to avoid loss or grief. What they fail to recognize, however, is that these feelings are a natural and normal part of life. When using Emotional Core Therapy to treat depression, golfers and clients must learn the proper coping mechanisms for processing grief. The time needed to heal varies from golfer to golfer and person to person. The severity of the situation makes a big difference. Losing a five-dollar bill is not going to cause as much as grief as finding out that you have cancer. The real problem with drowning your pain away or numbing yourself is that it does not work. It only delays the inevitable. At some point you have to fully grieve the loss.

Another major problem is that addictions dull the five senses, which then hampers our ability to identify the four authentic feelings. Take for example someone who has lost his job and then goes out and drinks eight beers a day for a month. This dulls ALL FOUR of the authentic feelings. Not only grief, which is what they intended to dull, but also joy, fear and relief. The whole body, including the muscular and skeletal system, will be adversely impacted. There is less chance of learning to identify authentic feelings, or to learn your body's responses, or how to relax. You can't work towards bringing more joy into your life, because you are numb. You also cannot effectively process feelings of grief. Day in and day out I hear of people, especially the young, who are told, "Take this drug or that drink and your pain will go away." ECT demonstrates the fallacy of this poor advice. The truth is, you are sabotaging your chance of recovering.

Emotional Core Therapy teaches us to calm the body by staying in a peaceful, meditative state throughout the day. By remaining this way for a prolonged period you can identify all fearful and toxic events in your life. This includes drugs or alcohol. A person that understands how a hot stove works would not touch it because they understand that it causes burns and pain. The same can be said for drugs and alcohol. Why would you use something that could cause legal and financial trouble? Why would you use something that could cause sensory deprivation?

None of this is to suggest that the causes of addiction, or treating them, are simple. There are many reasons why people do drugs: some do it for experimentation, others use it as a mild form of relaxation and there are many other reasons beyond those. With alcohol, a small amount can even be good for you, as can a glass of lemon tea. Yet there is a dramatic difference between four glasses of wine and four glasses of lemon tea! The wine drastically dulls your ability to experience the four authentic feelings. This is doubly destructive, because the more one dulls the senses, the less success ECT can achieve.

A relationship with drugs or any addiction can be very dangerous and can cause long-term damage to your system, especially highly addictive drugs such as cocaine. What can we do to alleviate the dangers? The more information one has about illicit drugs or alcohol, the less likely they will be to use them. Would someone really want to use methamphetamine (also known as "speed"), for example, if they knew the harm that it could cause to their body, or heroin, if they fully understood that an overdose could kill them? As if that weren't bad enough, with illegal drugs nobody knows exactly what is in it, meaning it often includes toxic substances that can be deadly. You need to notify your medical doctor when you have any mental health problems, but especially problems with addictions, because medical doctors have a good understanding of these issues (especially when harmful chemicals are involved) and how to address them. Over the years I have worked with a variety of addictions. This includes addictions to prescription drugs, cigarettes, alcohol, marijuana, narcotics, pornography, and junk food. ECT is a very helpful approach to addictions because it forces the client to examine all the relationships they are choosing to enter in their lives. When a client sees they are bringing fear and grief into their lives by acquiring an addiction they are more responsive to changing their behaviors. Why bring pain and suffering to your body along with possible legal and financial trouble? Why not work towards relationships that can bring you joy? An important point in treating addictions is to be kind and compassionate to the client suffering addiction. Anger pulls people away from communicating. When a therapist can bring up the dangers of a toxic relationship (such as most addictions) in a calm manner, the client is more receptive to learning. Oftentimes people need to get valuable information about addictions to make informed changes. It is very empowering for clients to make their own healthy decisions away from an addictive lifestyle. I often tell my clients that a healthy and supportive relationship with friends or family that can bring you joy is a great way to live.

Getting back specifically to ECT's treatment of depression, it can be very creative in the ways that it supports patients. For example, one woman I talked to remembered the classic song by The Fifth Dimension called, "One Less Bell to Answer." It's about a woman whose husband has left for good and she is emotionally devastated.

In her despair, she agonizes over why he had to leave. We talked about that song, and sometimes we even play songs in therapy as a tool. There is something soothing not only in the singer's heart-rending voice and words, but also in the song's rhythmic chorus and hauntingly smooth music. It helps relieve some of the grief to talk about whatever it is that hurts us, and it's a great way to help release feelings.

One of the reasons that music is such an excellent technique to release feelings is the sheer magnitude of songs. Some artist has recorded a song for nearly every possible type of relationship issue or problem. All four authentic feelings have hundreds, if not thousands of songs that people can relate to in every culture and virtually every personal situation. For example, consider the song, "All My Sorrows, Sad Tomorrows," by the group, The Marmalade. Its lyrics allow one to daydream and reflect on their own sorrowful past in a calm but sad manner.

Another tool might be to talk about movies, maybe a medical one. For instance, a client talked about a movie in which a man had to endure his young son's terrible illness, trying to find a cure for most of the movie. This drama was called "Lorenzo's Oil," and it was such a sad movie that it would bring tears to the viewers' eyes with the tragic sequence of events that unfold for the little boy. Another movie, "Ladder 49," was about a man dying in a fire. He was a very well liked fireman who was devoted to putting out fires. In this movie the rest of the firefighters, as well as the man's family and community, are devastated by the loss of his life. When a viewer watches this type of film it is possible to evoke some hidden feelings of loss. This kind of reading of toxic feelings happens to most of us daily in some fashion when we may be watching a soap opera or perhaps listening to a sad song on the car radio. None of this is meant to be morbid. The point is, hiding from grief does not make it go away and it does not cure depression. To the contrary, identifying the feelings of loss is the first step in coping with those feelings, and sometimes things like songs and movies can help us put our finger on the problem spot.

The one common factor in all of the examples we are discussing is that they are all about loss. But simply knowing that is not enough. We need to explore deeper, to get to the roots of what these relationships were truly about.

Another case I want to discuss where grief affected someone off the course was the case of an amateur golfer named Gary. He was a once a month golfer but that is not important in this case as we are highlighting his "real life stress" away from golf. When someone is seriously depressed like Gary, nearly all sporting activities will suffer.

Gary was a twenty-seven year old construction worker who had a girlfriend who he loved and adored. He worked for the family business, and the idea had been that he was supposed to make a lot of money following in his father's footsteps. But his father whom he worked for was very demanding. Moreover, the young man worked outside in the cold a lot, which he didn't really like at all.

In ECT therapy, we let him talk out his feelings. He shared things about himself, such as that when he was in high school he was a very good athlete. He was able to recognize and identify the things in life that brought him joy. These included working closely with people; he actually preferred to be working inside, not outside. As a matter of fact, he found great satisfaction working with customers.

Gary could not shake his depression until he changed several of his relationships, which were causing him grief. He was sad that he had to work underneath a demanding and mean spirited father. Gary was also sad that he had to work in an isolated job as a construction worker which meant he had to work more outside in cold weather with objects versus working with people inside in a warm office.

When Gary came to see me his level of sadness/depression was at an eight or nine! Gary had feelings of sadness that permeated throughout the day. He would start crying when no one was around. He would oversleep, lose hope, and isolate himself from friends. He also had trouble sleeping. Fortunately for Gary, he had the time and determination to alter his relationships that were causing him grief. Over the course of twelve months, he was able to quit his job and go back to school to be retrained. Gary came back to visit me a year after therapy ended to report that he had proudly earned employee of the month at his new, much happier job. His level of depression dropped from a nine to a one or two in just over a year. He performed better in all aspects of life, including golf.

Let's now try and examine Gary's case of depression through the eight step ECT Flowchart. The first step of the ECT Flowchart is realizing that entering and leaving relationships is what causes one stress. Relationship stress can occur with the relationship we have with ourselves, other people, places, or things. For Gary, Step One was recognizing that he entered into some new relationships with his father at work in the construction industry which were causing him stress.

Step Two of the ECT process is understanding that each relationship we enter into has various needs that have to be met. These needs are what causes one stress. The four categories of needs are emotional, financial, spiritual, and physical. Some relationships require only one or two of the four needs. Others may require all four needs. In Gary's case, the needs of the job were excessive for him. He was required to work long hours (physical) outside in the cold. He was yelled at (emotional) often by his father who didn't pay him very well (financial).

Step Three of the Eight Step Flowchart is understanding how our senses perceive stressful needs. Our five senses are hearing, touching, smelling, tasting, and seeing. This step happens quite automatically for most people, including Gary. He recognized his stress through hearing his dad yelling at him, touching the cold, and seeing his finances dwindle over time.

Step Four of the Eight Step Flowchart is examining which authentic feeling (joy, grief, fear, or relief) arises with the new relationship you have entered. In the case of Gary, he had immense grief from his working relationship with his dad's company. Although their were many aspects of the work relationship that caused him grief, the cold weather, lack of pay, and anger he felt from his dad, were all sources of grief.

Step Five of the ECT Flowchart is when these emotions get sent to our brain, which is part of the central nervous system. The central nervous system sends messages to our muscular and skeletal system. This step happens automatically for almost all people, including Gary.

Step Six is understanding how these uncomfortable symptoms affect our body in the form of muscle tension and tightness, etc. Gary recognized the oversleeping, the loss of hope, and crying spells as signs of stress.

Step Seven of the ECT process is the releasing process. Learning to discharge toxic emotions. In Gary's case we used many types of techniques to release emotions. One that was very effective was daily journaling, where he wrote down exactly what he felt each day.

Step Eight of the ECT process was balancing your equilibrium and practicing your daily meditative exercises. For Gary, he used daily swimming at the health club as a time to regroup and calm himself down. When Gary swam, he was able to get his stress out of his body and feel warm and relaxed.

As I mentioned earlier in the book, the ECT process and Flowchart can be used successfully to identify and process any future stress you encounter in life. There has rarely been a human encounter that I can't comprehend using ECT. On rare occasions, the external relationships we enter into are multiple in a short period of time so it is hard to distinguish which needs exactly caused you stress. For example, jogging on a hot, humid day and stopping off for a burrito. When eating your burrito you put extra hot sauce on it and down a liter of Pepsi. Afterwards you feel terrible and have excess grief. It may not be possible to pin down exactly what caused your stomach to be upset and for you to feel grief. The important aspect to remember is that your true feeling is grief so you won't be repeating that behavior anytime soon!

Once you learn ECT you will have the confidence needed to pick healthy relationships in your life. It takes repetition and practice but the benefits far outweigh the effort needed to learn ECT. As you read the cases presented throughout the rest of the book, keep the ECT process in your mind. Try and visualize each step that the characters in the book are engaging in their stressful scenarios. ECT can also be used to examine any routine stress such as throwing out your back lifting a heavy object or missing a free throw in basketball. As a reminder, ECT is the only psychological approach, religious teaching, or educational approach that can successfully release the root cause of relationship stress without redirecting your emotions away from how you truly feel. Our four true emotions help us navigate our way on the golf course and in life. The more we can learn about these four emotions, the easier time we will have choosing healthy relationships on and off the course that make us happy. With ECT, we now have a process that can successfully treat the situational stress that weakens golfers and human beings from time to time. ECT can treat this stress effectively because it addresses the root cause of the problem, which is the arousal of one of the four true feelings. We are now ready to explore how the authentic feeling of fear helps and hurts golfers in the upcoming chapter.

List Five Relationships That Have Brought You Grief on the Golf Course

A) HITTING THE BALL IN THE WATER

B) SHANKING A GOLF SHOT

1)

2)

3)

4)

5)

NOTES:

List Five Ways You Can Release Feelings Of Grief on and Off the Golf Course

A) JOURNALING

B) DEEP BREATHING

1)

2)

3)

4)

5)

Symptoms Of Loss and Grief On and Off the Golf Course

Crying spells for no apparent reason

Loss of interest or pleasure in normal activities

Changes in appetite

Fatigue, tiredness and loss of energy

Feelings of sadness or unhappiness

Irritability or frustration, even over small matters

Indecisiveness, distractibility and decreased concentration

List Five Of Your Own Symptoms Of Grief and Loss On and Off the Golf Course

1)

2)

3)

4)

5)

NOTES:

ECT Flow Chart

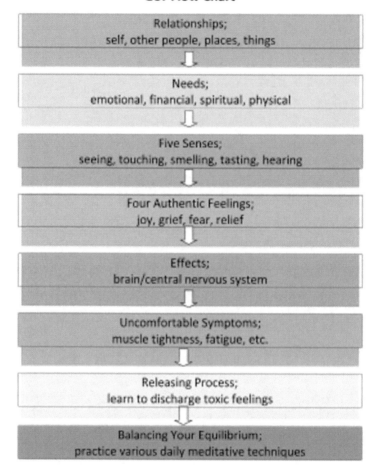

Relationships;
self, other people, places, things

Needs;
emotional, financial, spiritual, physical

Five Senses;
seeing, touching, smelling, tasting, hearing

Four Authentic Feelings;
joy, grief, fear, relief

Effects;
brain/central nervous system

Uncomfortable Symptoms;
muscle tightness, fatigue, etc.

Releasing Process;
learn to discharge toxic feelings

Balancing Your Equilibrium;
practice various daily meditative techniques

CHAPTER FOUR
Helping Golfers with Fear/Anxiety

As we begin this chapter on fear/anxiety I want to discuss an important aspect of emotional power. What really makes a golfer strong mentally? Why do some of the elite players look so comfortable and confident over the ball in pressure-packed situations? The answer is preparation. The elite golfers spend hours on the driving range and chipping/putting greens fine tuning their game. They work out all the kinks in their swings off the course and then take their perfected swing on the course. Elite golfers have a smaller variance in their shots compared to amateurs. They truly enjoy the vast majority of their swings. For the most part, elite golfers are readily aware that they have an elite game. One of the dynamics the TV cameras don't show is the hours upon hours of preparation it takes to get to that level. That preparation lessens the chance of tension and poor shots.

Whether you are an amateur or professional, ECT can help you get the most out of your golf game by giving you invaluable feedback on your shots. The golf course does not lie. After several rounds of golf the golf course will expose most any flaw a golfer has in their golf game. The key for any golfer is to master these ten aspects of the game:

1. Effective Driver off the tee. Most 18-hole golf courses require 10-14 shots with the driver.
2. Effective long (hybrid and 3,4,5 iron) and short iron (6,7,8,9, pitching wedge, sand wedge, lob wedge) game.
3. Effective bunker game. Both fairway and green side bunker.
4. Effective chipping and pitching game when near the green.
5. Effective putting.

6. Effective mental game to cope with the ups and downs of golf.
7. Be in good physical shape to swing all the clubs effectively.
8. Have the financial resources to play golf and get the coaching you need to compete.
9. Have the time to play and practice golf, including optimal weather conditions.
10. Have a solid support system in place that will reward you for playing well. This includes friends, family, etc.

Nearly all amateur and professional golfers struggle with one, two or more aspects of these ten important categories. Some of these categories can change from time to time. For example, injuries can suddenly hinder a golfer, as can an unexpected financial disaster. All of these aspects of the game can cause a golfer situational stress. This results in the arousal of the true and authentic feeling of fear. Other synonyms for fear that you likely know are anxiety or dread. The emotion is caused by going towards something you dislike. This chapter will focus on how *to learn* from fear rather than having fear adversely affect your golf game.

The first case of fear I would like to mention is that of Sandra. She was an amateur golfer I worked with for a few months to help with her mental game of golf. She was a 12-handicap golfer who loved the game. Overall her golf game was pretty balanced except for a few intricate parts. The focus of this case was her green side sand bunker game. As we discussed earlier, each shot in golf is viewed as a separate and distinct relationship. The focus of ECT is to take ownership of each golf shot and learn from each shot.

For a 12 handicapper, Sandra was below average in all aspects of her sand bunker game. She was not confident she would get the ball on the green from an uphill or flat lie in the bunker. Worse yet, from a downward sloping green side bunker, Sandra would badly botch the shot causing her to score very poorly. Landing in the bunker meant a bogie or worse for Sandra every time. Sometimes she'd get a double or triple bogie when she was in the bunker, which, of course, would ruin an otherwise good round.

In observing Sandra, I noticed some obvious technical flaws with her golf swing in the bunker. Besides poor mechanics, and because of rushing, Sandra would hurry her backswing. To the naked eye, it would look like she was having a minor panic attack before the tough shot. Sandra would display symptoms of angst, tightness in her shoulders and sweaty palms. What was happening in reality was a combination of things. She was overly fearful of her shots out of the bunker. This excess fear caused her central nervous system to be elevated. Having an elevated central nervous system meant excess energy was being used for her shot. Why? With an elevated CNS a golfer has excess blood, water, and oxygen flowing into their muscles. Golf requires a fluid swing and excellent timing. This is especially important out of bunkers where a mis-hit can mean you still have to repeat the bunker shot.

Sandra worked with a golf pro to improve her scoring from the bunker and other tough spots. Again, I encourage anyone struggling with the technical aspects of a golf swing to talk to a teaching golf pro who teaches all aspects of the game. Whatever type of golf shot one hits, there exist multiple ways to execute it. Look at any professional golf tournament where over a hundred and fifty professionals are entered. You will see five to ten variations on most golf shots. For example, something as simple as a putting stroke. You will see long clubs, short clubs, thick grips, thin grips, smooth strokes, firm strokes, etc. The key is they are effective, for the most part on the professional tour.

Over the course of six weeks Sandra was able to find a golf swing that effectively landed the ball on or near the green. She improved her bunker game because she had the ability to accept feedback from others, including her mental and technical coaches. Sandra was able to be a calm and easy-going person off the golf course. She disliked feeling uncomfortable emotionally. To finally find a resolution to her excessive fear surrounding her bunker game was a great relief for her. As I mentioned to Sandra and all my clients on and off the golf course, when you can stay relaxed and stable, your mind and body will help you if you allow them to by identifying core emotions. It can feel very uncomfortable on the golf course to go through five to ten minutes of acute stress and bodily discomfort while playing. For Sandra, the more comfortable she became with her new golf swing out of the bunker, the less she displayed excessive fear or anxiety. Once my golfers and other clients master ECT, they have the full confidence they can handle any future stress on or off the golf course! Why? ECT works to identify and process any relationship stress. Once you feel bodily discomfort like Sandra, you can go the Eight Step ECT Flowchart and process your stress effectively and completely. No other psychology approach, religious teaching, or educational teaching can do this as effectively.

Now let's break down Sandra's stress in the sand bunker using the ECT Flowchart. Remember once you learn ECT, you can usually process these golf shots rather quickly.

The first step of the ECT Flowchart is understanding that entering and leaving relationships is what causes stress. These can be relationships with ourselves, other people, places, or things like golf shots. In Sandra's case, she hit a golf ball into a sand bunker. Each golf shot is a separate and unique relationship.

The second step of the ECT Flowchart is to recognize that each new relationship requires needs to be met. These cause stress to golfers as well as all people. Needs are broken down into four categories. Emotional, financial, spiritual, and physical. Generally speaking, with golfers, we usually focus on the physical needs/demands of the golf course. In Sandra's case, she had to meet the demands of hitting a golf ball from tricky lies/sloping lies with sand underneath instead of grass.

The third step of the ECT Flowchart is understanding that we perceive these needs through our five senses. Hearing, touching, smelling, tasting, and seeing. This step happens quite automatically for almost all golfers, including Sandra. She used her sense of sight to get a view of the slope and the golf ball. She used her sense of touch to grip her club and take her firm stance in the bunker.

Step Four of the ECT Flowchart is understanding that one of our four authentic feelings, joy, grief, fear, or relief, is aroused when we enter into every new relationship. In Sandra's case of her excess stress/mini panic attacks, she had a gnawing fear when she was in the bunker. Because of her poor technique, this fear was often prolonged as it would take several shots to get out of the bunker. Although there are many names for fear (anxiety, dread, terrified, etc) it is critically important to understand the true emotion of fear. Fear comes from going towards something you dislike. For all golfers, including Sandra, fear is with us hourly and daily our whole lives. The secret to life, so to speak, is to minimize or eliminate those relationships that cause us fear. Why? Our central nervous system is aroused when we sense fear. A heightened CNS is not a healthy way to live.

Step Five is to recognize that these four authentic emotions are introduced to us through our CNS. The CNS is the brain which then sends messages to our muscular skeletal system, which is what controls our golf shots. This step happens automatically for all golfers, including Sandra.

Step Six is to identify the symptoms, sometimes uncomfortable, that cause us bodily tension. When Sandra was in the bunker she had felt her heart racing, tightness in her chest, and sweaty palms.

Step Seven of the ECT Flowchart is "the releasing process". Learning to discharge uncomfortable and debilitating emotions. Any psychological technique that can successfully release emotions can be incorporated into ECT. The key for golfers is to find something short and sweet that works for you on the golf course. Sandra and I worked on doing some light stretches in between golf shots. Just a few leg extensions and hip extension stretches she was able to accomplish in 30 seconds or so. When she was really stressed, she would repeat the stretches till she calmed down. Stretching became a way for Sandra to soothe herself and let her uncomfortable thoughts and emotions dissipate throughout her body. Stretching also helped to oxygenate the joints and muscles and keep her fresh for the entire round.

Step Eight is to balance your equilibrium and practice daily meditative techniques. Even something as subtle as walking the golf course versus riding a golf cart may improve a golfer's ability to relax and meditate. On the course, we are trying to calm and quiet the mind. When we do this, we have a better chance of identifying stress. In Sandra's case she decided to take extra time over her putts and chips as a way to slow down her psyche. By reading both sides of the putt and chip, she would do more walking and found that this calmed her down.

Another case of anxiety/excess fear on the golf course was with an amateur golfer named Fred. Fred had a stressful job as a lawyer and a passion for golf. The problem was that he would carry his stress from work to the golf course. His mind seemed to be going a million miles an hour at all times. Occasionally, Fred's forearms would tighten and he would clench his wrists when chipping or putting. When I would watch Fred play, I noted that he would rush his backswing on many of his drives and iron shots. Oftentimes, when putting, he would not take his time and align a putt. Usually, when he missed a shorter putt, he would quickly stand over the ball and hastily putt again. This meant several three putts a round. It was clear to me in my assessment of Fred, that he was "pretty stressed out" both on and off the golf course. What does the term "stressed out" mean in the context of Fred's life as a lawyer and his golf game? Fred has excess fear related to his tasks at work and in golf. Everyone perceives stress differently. Another man may very well be able to do Fred's job and golf in a relaxed manner. No two people are alike in how they perceive stress.

Let's take a closer look at one aspect (of many) of Fred's golf game that caused him stress and lost golf shots on the course. Several times a round, Fred would not align his chips or putts. Rather, he would walk up to the golf ball with a sour look on his face. He would set up rather quickly and take his chip or putt. This caused him to lose two to four shots at least every round. Although he carried his stress inappropriately throughout a good portion of the day, we only have time to focus on this aspect here in the book.

What was Fred doing wrong with his chips and putts? How was he letting his emotions hurt him versus help him on the golf course? Well, let's look at an effective way to chip or putt. I am not speaking of mechanical or technical aspects of both chipping and putting in this instance. Fred, like most decent amateur golfers had a chipping and putting stroke that was efficient. As I mentioned throughout the book, ECT examines the mental aspect of golf. Questions regarding the technical/mechanical aspects of the swing are best suited for a teaching professional. What was obvious from the naked eye was that when Fred was anxious he would not properly align his chips or putts. He would not look at the proper slope of the green when he was in a hurry. Fred would also swing his club a tad quicker on his chips and putts. This behavior would happen, according to Fred two to three times during his 18 hole round of golf.

When working with Fred over a twelve-week period we examined his mental approach from tee to green for all 18 holes. We looked at his pre-shot routine and his post-shot routine. We looked at how he carried himself in between his golf shots and in between holes on the course. In all those areas we reviewed what he was thinking and feeling. Was his mental approach to golf helping or hurting him.

The first point I observed when working with Fred was his lack of a relaxed mindset on the golf course. Psychology has grown and evolved over the last 30 years and one of the trendiest techniques in the field is what is called "Mindfulness." Many successful therapy approaches utilize mindfulness as a beginning point in their psychology kit of successful techniques. ECT does not use mindfulness, but rather an approach that is very similar. With ECT, I teach all my golfers, athletes, and clients to learn to have a relaxed, daydreaming, meditative mindset. Where your mind is allowed to wander, free float, and daydream. The ability to do this is within all of us! The vast majority of humans do this for at least a small portion of the day. For example, think about when you wake up in the morning and are brushing your teeth or showering. With our relaxed mindset we are not thinking or using cognition. Thinking and cognition require you to think about relationships. Invariably, when you think about relationships, your CNS gets elevated. We don't want this when we are trying to relax.

In Fred's case we first worked on relaxing off the golf course using what is called "spa music". Spa music is what you hear when you go to a massage parlor or in a doctor's office waiting room. It sounds like elevator music. No words, just soothing sounds like water going over rocks, firewood crackling on your fireplace, jazzy sounds, soft and soothing musical instruments. When Fred was in his law office doing paperwork, he would have a CD player in the background playing soft music. We then worked to implement this mood on the golf course. Fred would hum the beats he memorized from listening to them throughout the day.

Fred learned to sing to himself in a quiet manner that did not disrupt his playing partners. When Fred was on the driving range, he would have his headset on relaxing while hitting shots. We also implemented this humming to himself over his chips and putts. Over time Fred began to grasp the fact that each shot in golf is a separate relationship. Each shot was going to evoke a separate feeling from him. By learning to honor those feelings he would have a better chance of learning from them. Slowing down his golf game and life would allow him to make healthy relationships in all aspects of his life.

For Fred, when he slowed his mannerisms down on the golf course, he began to have a better appreciation of the game. He had been cheating himself by saying he didn't care about the short chips or putts and that was why he previously rushed through them. Now, after learning and applying ECT, he began to value each shot. Fred would read both sides of the cup when chipping and putting. He would learn the slopes of each green before he chipped or putted a ball. Over time, he shaved strokes off his scorecard as he began to learn what it was to properly hit a chip or putt. It was no longer a grip and rip attitude, but rather a slow methodical approach that a serious tactician of the short game around the greens displayed.

As I explained to Fred, he had been deceiving himself/lying to himself that these chips and putts around the green did not matter to him. When we examined Fred's thinking immediately prior to hitting these shots the emotion of "fear" came up. Fred was scared of these shorter-range shots. Why? They usually shocked him when he missed them and he would be upset for five to fifteen minutes afterwards. By pretending he didn't care, it seemed easier for Fred to just ignore the pain he was feeling. Sometimes, during a round, Fred would drink beer or smoke a cigarette to numb his pain. The problem with this poor coping mechanism, Fred would find out, was that it didn't work. Why? Numbing himself up in between shots didn't help him learn about his golf game. Also, he was delaying his emotional growth on the golf course.

As I told to Fred, the four true feelings (joy, grief, fear, and relief) are with us shot by shot on the golf course. They are also with us hourly and daily off the golf course. The feeling of joy, although temporary, is what drives humans to achieve both on the golf course and off the golf course. "Wasn't this something you valued, Fred?" I asked.

"Of course," Fred replied. Soon, he was on his way to becoming a better golfer and a more authentic human being. Remember, as a reader, to try and apply ECT to each of the golf shots that have caused you stress. Over time, you will become more accustomed to the ECT process and Flowchart. Remember, ECT can also be used for any other sporting event (basketball, archery, tennis, etc) or life event (parenting, addictions to shopping or caffeine, eating disorders, etc). Take your time and try and visualize any stress in your sporting or real life with ECT. Are you getting the hang of ECT yet? If not, don't worry, we will help you become a master by the end of the book. It just takes time and will. Both are resources we have within us all as human beings.

Now let's look at the eight step ECT Flowchart and see how Fred was able to utilize ECT to help his golf game. The first step of ECT was recognizing that relationships either come together or grow apart. This is what causes stress to golfers. For Fred, recognizing that each chip and putt was a new relationship with new opportunities was his first step.

The second step of the ECT Flowchart is to understand that each new relationship requires needs to be met. These needs are what cause golfers stress. Needs are broken down into four categories. Emotional, financial, spiritual, and physical. It is important to note that a majority of the needs/demands that a golfer faces on a golf course are physical. For example, the need to strike your driver 260 yards to have a shot at the green on a par four hole.

An interesting point to make regarding needs is that they can change from time to time and cause us more stress. For example, one day your golf course is looking great for scoring. The weather is warm and the sun is shining. You are playing in excellent weather conditions.

The next day it is cold and rainy causing you to play miserably on the same course. This is similar to life. One day, your five year old is smiling and drawing cute pictures for his parents. The next day, the same child has a temper tantrum. This same child has an entirely different set of needs on a day to day basis. For Fred, the uncertain slope of the greens was a relationship he entered into that caused him duress on the golf course.

The third step of the ECT process and Flowchart is that golfers perceive these stressful needs through the five senses. Our five senses are seeing, touching, smelling, tasting, hearing. This step happens automatically for nearly all golfers. For Fred, he would use his sense of sight to see the green for his chips and putts. Fred would use his sense of touch to feel his clubs when he hit his golf shots around the green.

The fourth step of the ECT Flowchart is to understand which one of the four authentic feelings has arisen because of the golfer's new stressful encounter. In Fred's case, when he was near the green chipping or putting, he often had the authentic feeling of excessive, unreasonable fear .

The fifth step is an automatic step for golfers in that your authentic feelings send messages to your brain, which is part of the central nervous system. The brain sends messages to the muscular and skeletal system, which allows your muscles to execute the golf shot. This step occurred automatically for Fred, like most golfers.

Step Six is the identification of stress step. We learn which arousal/uncomfortable symptoms of stress was caused by our authentic feelings. Fred exhibited symptoms of stress such as racing thoughts, tightness in his forearms, and clenching his wrists before some chips or putts. This would happen intermittently throughout the round of golf.

Step Seven of the ECT Flowchart is the releasing process. Learning to discharge the sometimes toxic emotions of the four feelings when they arise. In Fred's case the excess fear he displayed over his chipping and putting was harmful to his golf game. We focused on having

Fred write down how he felt after each hole on the golf course. Because it was too difficult to write down each of his emotions after each golf shot, we needed to do something practical and effective in the short-term to help his golf game. By writing down his emotions after each hole, Fred was learning to monitor his emotions. He was becoming more aware of how he felt on the course. He was learning to honor his true emotions on the golf course. Like many of my golfers, Fred, was able to use what he learned on the golf course in real life. He kept a journal by his bed and would write down whatever he was thinking before he turned in for the night. This helped clear his mind before he went to sleep. For the majority of my clients, verbalizing how one feels and writing these emotions down can go a long way towards recovery from stress.

Step Eight of the ECT process is balancing your equilibrium. Practicing daily meditative exercises. For Fred, humming and singing to himself seemed to calm him down during his golf round. He would listen to his spa music both in the office and at home. As I mentioned in the beginning of this book, ECT is the most inclusive psychology approach in the world for golfers and all people. Why? ECT allows you to self sooth in ways that fit your lifestyle. For some golfers, walking the dog, gardening, or watching movies may be a way to comfort and relax the mind. Everyone is different. The key is to have your mind not thinking about much. Let it wander, free float, and daydream. When you do this, you are learning to love and protect yourself. When you are calm, your CNS is calm. It then becomes easier to identify and release the stress associated with the arousal of the four true feelings of joy, grief, fear, and relief.

Before we talk about our next golfer, Kevin, I want to clarify one more point regarding ECT. The goal of ECT is emotional empowerment. I want each golfer to feel hopeful, optimistic, and energetic over each golf shot he is about to hit. This can only occur when you have fully released your emotions. Oftentimes, the four feelings are barely noticeable when you are playing. Many golfers have a decent idea of how they are playing and sometimes only get aroused every couple of holes. Every golfer is unique. So properly assessing your game is the first step in mastering the psychology of golf.

Kevin was a high school golfer who carried a five handicap. Very solid in nearly all aspects of the game, Kevin, for the most part, was a very confident golfer. When he would play alone, or with friends, he was usually at his best. The problem for Kevin would arise when he would play competitive golf for his high school team. Occasionally, he would feel very stressed and shoot ten to twelve over par for 18 holes. This was usually five to seven shots he lost because of his poor mental approach to golf. Worse than his golf shots was how Kevin felt after his poor golfing. He would get depressed and sad and that uncomfortable feeling would last a day or two.

Let's look closer at what was really going on with Kevin. This time, instead of me highlighting the steps to ECT, see if you can figure them out on your own. Remember, the way to master the mind is to both learn and apply the ECT process to your own life. By actively using your mind you will have a better chance of retaining the information in this book. That is why I also recommend doing all the exercises at the end of each chapter.

Kevin had excessive anxiety/fear when he played competitively. Competitive golf for Kevin meant new people were involved in his golf game. His girlfriend and parents would come and watch his matches. His close friends Tommy and Joe were also on the golf team. The coach would make a big deal out of beating the opponents and winning the conference championship. All these extra variables became overwhelming for Kevin occasionally. When he would stand over a drive on the tee box he would think, *Is my girlfriend watching? What if I mis-hit the ball?* When he was hitting some of his approach shots into the green, he was wondering, *If I miss this badly, will our team lose?* Sometimes, when he putted the ball, he said aloud, "Man, will I look good to my parents or friends if I make this putt!"

What was problematic about Kevin's golf game mentally? He was allowing too many hypothetical relationship stresses to enter into his mind. These relationship thoughts caused Fred excessive fear resulting in his central nervous system being elevated. Worse yet, he felt horrible after playing poorly and this meant not getting the most out of his day off the golf course. As I explained to Kevin, a calm CNS was essential before each golf shot! Why? We are asking our body and mind to do many things as a golfer. Some of these tasks vary in their complexity. Sometimes we need to swing hard, sometimes very softly. When you are overwhelmed your swing will suffer from too much adrenaline affecting your muscles. Think of it this way, what if a boxer or MMA fighter thought about all those things Kevin thought about on the golf course while in the ring fighting? What if immediately before he swung his fists he thought of his girlfriend or parents? He would likely get punched, lambasted and smacked down in the ring. Too much cognition is rarely effective for any athlete. The focus for each golf shot is preparation and execution. It is important to empty the mind from all undue relationship stress on the golf course. Although you won't get knocked out like a boxer who thinks too much in the ring, the pain of throwing strokes away hurts in some way.

My training with Kevin first dealt with allowing the mind to fully relax before each shot. I had Kevin tell me what he was thinking before some of his shots. We discussed how having these thoughts caused him excessive fear or anxiety. Kevin and I worked though the entire ECT process prior to starting to address his issues on the golf course. As with all my clients, I articulate a clear plan of action after first assessing the problem. Kevin felt fully confident in the process.

Kevin and I discussed how having any extraneous thoughts while golfing can be harmful to your game. Much of the mental aspect of golf is learning to empty the mind after each golf shot, just like emptying the trash. Good or bad thoughts have to be released quickly after each shot. Think again of a trash compactor. You have some good food and bad food in the refrigerator. Out the trash goes every day, just like ridding yourself of whatever of the four emotions you are harboring (joy, grief, fear, and relief).

Kevin and I used some of the techniques previously mentioned in this book. On the golf course, players are limited in what they can use to release emotions. When Kevin was practicing, he would listen to quiet, upbeat music on his headphones. He worked on his breathing to make sure he had slow deep breaths. Kevin would often sit under a tree when he wasn't playing and do light stretching. He would say a few positive affirmations that we talked about in sessions such as, "Golf is something I chose to do. I excel at golf. I am a good person. I will love myself whether I hit a good shot or bad shot." Over time, Kevin started to believe in himself. Kevin and I discussed how whenever he would feel tension prior to swinging, he would regroup. He would regroup by stepping away from his golf stance. Look at the sky and trees. Take a few breaths till he felt calm and quiet. We worked towards getting a feel and routine just like he had on the practice driving range where he felt no pressure at all. It takes time to relearn proper psychology techniques. There is usually some regression and mistakes along the way. All the more reason to be kind to yourself while learning something new.

As we discuss the aspect of learning ECT for off the course stresses I want to remind my fellow golfers how the mind works. The identification, processing, and releasing of emotions are learned behaviors. Much like learning to use all the various clubs in your golf bag, learning to understand how the brain, mind, and body interact with the environment takes time and repetition to fully work effectively.

Let's take a look at a high school freshman girl who takes golf with her gym class at school for several weeks in the fall of her school year. This young girl has never touched a golf club in her life. After two weeks of gym class with the golf instructor the class ends. Then the following summer, she is asked to pick up her clubs and head to the golf course without any warning and play 18 holes. This would be a very arduous task for any young student athlete. Why? There is a sequence and process to learning how to play a full round of golf. No one in their right mind would expect this young lady to fully remember all the tasks at hand she learned eight months prior in gym class. The same is true in matters of the mind. "Use it or lose it" is the saying for golf instructors when teaching a certain swing. Ditto for emotions. Emotions are with us hourly and daily our whole lives. If we are not tuned into our emotions off the golf course we will forget how to use them. A deeper question needs to be asked at this time. Since the authentic emotions help navigate us to live peaceful and happy lives, would we ever want to forget how they work? The answer is obviously no! We never want to forget how our emotional compass works off the golf course or on the golf course. Our four feelings are meant to protect us and give us real lasting emotional power. In many ways, the stronger we feel off the course, the more likely we are going to perform on the course. Why? We learn to train better so we don't get injured. We learn to eat a healthy lifestyle so we have proper nutrition. We learn to build healthy and supportive relationships that can improve our golf game and life. Let's now turn to some examples from outside the game of golf where ECT has made a tremendous impact on people's lives.

The first example that we use involves a young man in his early twenties named Drew. He came to my office complaining of feeling scared about his life. He was nervous that he was not his usual self. He was terrified that he was not living up to being a man. He joined the military, but once he got to boot camp he had a difficult time fulfilling the rigorous requirements and ultimately dropped out. Drew became worried about his self-esteem, and he felt weak for not being able to successfully complete boot camp. The experience was very demanding on the young recruit. The drill instructor was mean spirited, hostile and angry all day long. Drew would wake up at the crack of dawn with the drill instructor yelling at him. He would then be ordered around all day and night by this very demanding guy. Drew was pushed to his limits both physically and mentally during his thirty-day ordeal that included shooting guns off, sleep-deprivation, hot sun, and severe weather conditions.

When we examine some of the feelings that Drew faced we see that he used words such as terrified, nervous and scared. The primary feeling was fear – especially of failing family and friends. Some of Drew's symptoms included a loss of attention, lack of sleep, lack of concentration and fatigue. These are all classic examples of someone who is suffering from fear and anxiety.

For Drew a full recovery would occur within a few months of the counseling. A supportive environment for him to release his feelings of fear would be paramount to his recovery. The focus of treatment would be releasing Drew's traumatic experience. I emphasize traumatic because each situation is different for each individual. For example, there were young men in Drew's boot camp class who were able to successfully graduate without any psychological stress. Some people perceive situations as more stressful than others. So we have to honor each person's fear and how it impacts them.

Part of Drew's success in counseling was that he was able to fully express all the harmful events that happened to him. Moreover, because of his time in the counseling office, he learned that it was okay to express what was on his mind. In fact, it was very important to his recovery.

With Emotional Core Therapy, an accepting and non-judgmental ambience is essential in order to trust the process. Even the most horrendous thoughts or feelings are allowed to be expressed, whether they are accurate or not. We sort those out. I gave Drew several examples to practice releasing feelings at home. He was able to choose from a variety of ways to release his feelings. That's what we do with all of our clients. We give them the option to choose what they want to do based on their own world experience and what they like to do.

Some of the ideas include writing, journaling, drawing, listening to music, exercising, jogging, meditation, yoga, or Pilates to name a few. Drew began to feel comfortable in therapy because he chose to freely verbalize his feelings. He started to do more talking, too, which he wasn't used to doing at home, where his family didn't really support expressing his feelings. Once he got into therapy, Drew became more expressive and he started to like it.

Every client is different in how they choose to express themselves. The best way for a therapist to do ECT is to work from a client's perspective and worldview. For Drew, learning to verbalize his unwanted feelings was a huge emotional growth step. He realized over time that it was okay to talk about negative feelings and to show his vulnerabilities. Drew also began to realize the value of cathartically releasing his feelings. He learned how to self-monitor his body for changes in his physical state, and realized that he was getting better as he started to release his feelings. Consequently, his fear level went down.

To examine how ECT helped Drew recover in this situation let's go back to the diagram in Chapter One on authentic feelings. Our brain receives authentic feelings such as fear. Once our brain, which is part of our central nervous system, senses these feelings, the muscles in our body respond. This sequence of events is helpful for our survival as human beings. If one is having trouble understanding this concept think of a situation which has occurred to most of us at home, touching a hot stove. If you accidentally touch a hot stove and burn your finger, you are not likely to repeat this mistake again. Why? We

sense the fear as a result of the negative conse-
quence that the action has on our body, i.e., a
burnt finger and the accompanying pain. As for
Drew, in therapy he learned to monitor his body
and to pay attention to his body's feelings. The
symptoms that he experienced were not normal
so we try to pay attention to those and over time
monitor their slowly dissipating.

Another step in Drew's recovery was the
use of meditation and relaxation in his life on
a daily basis. Drew had nightmares for months
prior to entering therapy so it was important for
him to learn to have a quiet state of being as part
of his daily life. Every person in therapy relaxes
in a different way. One person may like sitting
in a Jacuzzi, while someone else might like yoga
or Pilates, and others might like to do relaxing
activities like bowling or walking a dog. The key
to relaxing is to have the mind be free of tension, to be able to daydream, to reflect and be
able to stay calm. The key is to have a low level
of cognition. Cognition is where you are actually
thinking and using your mind actively. We don't
want that; we want the mind to freely flow and

to reflect. This differs for each person because each person relaxes in a different way. Another term for relaxation is self-soothing. Everybody self-soothes in different ways so we have to go to their point of view. When we talk about different techniques of relaxation, what's good for one person is not necessarily good for another.

Let's take sewing for example. One person may find sewing relaxing and they can release feelings that way. But another person may find sewing very stressful because it's physically taxing or they may not know how to do it.

So you have to really pay attention to what each person feels helps his or her mind to relax. We have to go back to their history of what they did when they were younger to relax, and we always give people the option of what they want to do to relax. When we examined Drew's history we found that he enjoyed sitting in his room listening to music. While listening to different artists express themselves and their feelings Drew slowly felt his tensions easing away. This process, however, takes time. Once Drew was able to see how authentic feelings operate, he began to release his feelings. His recovery started when he realized that he didn't have to enter boot camp anymore. That was a situation and a relationship that he had entered into but it was separate from himself and he realized that he would never have to go back to it again. That was an important step for him and a critical component of Emotional Core Therapy, realizing that all relationships either grow or die. He realized that his relationship with boot camp was in the past, that he was separate from that and he could now start to release that fear. By doing this, Drew was finally able to take back control over his life. Once he understood that he was over this experience he could start to release the pain of it.

All the experiences that Drew had gone through in boot camp were separate from himself. He entered into these relationships and he left them. In therapy, he was reminded that he succeeded in other events. So why not this event?

Another key for Drew was releasing pain through nature. Things such as trees and water, open land and spaces help the mind to daydream and wander. With ECT, a client like Drew does not have to be alone, he has an expert therapist side by side helping him sort out his traumatic feelings. Almost certainly Drew would be overwhelmed at the onset of therapy. On a daily basis the sorting out and releasing of his debilitating feelings of fear and loss would help to calm him down and get him back to a balanced equilibrium.

One question we need to ask is why would Drew not be able to release his feelings? With ECT we recognize that the body has a way of protecting itself from foreign or outside feelings. It is not normal and healthy to have debilitating feelings of fear and loss in our lives. If you don't believe what I'm saying, envision a two-year-old girl or boy in a crib. If a two-year-old child has suffered the psychological pain of being yelled at or scolded constantly what would happen? By the same token what would happen if this two-year-old was in his yard and a strange dog came up barking in his face? Quite naturally, the child would start crying to show fear. The child would show visible pain and look for comfort. What would be the remedy? Quite possibly it would be a loving hug from Mommy or Daddy or to take the boy away from the dog or the yard where the fearful event had occurred. If bitten, maybe a Band-Aid to stop the bleeding or a visit to the doctor for a shot to make sure that there are no diseases of infections. Every normal and healthy parent would do all that they could to help the child in pain. Why? Because a child cannot do these things themselves, and a two-year-old child cannot lie and deceive themselves about how they feel. They cannot hide pain. They have to release it somehow.

It is a natural process to release emotional pain by crying and whining. They have no defense mechanisms to block the cognitive emotions. Every loving parent would do whatever they could to protect this two-year-old and quite naturally console their pain. Why? The parent loves the child. It is a very powerful relationship. This same power of love is what has to transpire for Drew to get better. He has to respect himself enough to cheer himself and allow himself to get better. It was not a short process for full recovery but so long as Drew had the support of people around him a full recovery was expected. You see, the human body has a natural way of protecting us from danger. The psychological angst of sustaining things like fear and loss is dangerous to the human body. Drew has to allow himself to be held, comforted, and supported to be protected, just like this two-year-old. He has to respect himself and his feelings enough to allow himself to heal from this pain.

Another off the golf course case of anxiety/fear involves a successful mortgage specialist who owned a small company. William was divorced for a long time before he met his new wife, Kathy. Together they decided to start a family. Kathy already had one boy prior to meeting William. William had been quite happy with his life the previous ten years before he met Kathy and liked who he was as a person. When he came to my office in a panic, he was in a minor meltdown. He didn't know what the problem was with himself, and he felt like he was falling apart. He couldn't sleep, he couldn't concentrate, had trouble eating and he couldn't feel comfortable around people anymore. He couldn't even be intimate with his wife because he was so stressed out. His level of fear on a scale of one to ten was a nine or ten, in other words, intolerable. So I recommended like I do to all my clients to see a medical doctor when they enter therapy and the doctor can decide whether or not medical treatment is needed. With any counseling whether it's ECT or some other form of therapy, you want to make sure their doctor is notified if they desire it. Some will say they do not want to do so, while others will say that's fine. In William's case, he did not want to take medication even though he was having trouble sleeping. But it was important to get his sleeping in order so that he could start to recuperate because sleep is a recuperative process that you need to reinvigorate yourself. So for a short time William was on medication so that he could sleep better and calm himself down. He was adamant, however, that he didn't want to be on medication long term.

William was a very intelligent man who was able to identify his authentic feelings pretty quickly in his first couple of months of therapy, along with the real cause of his stress. After a brief examination of his life he saw that he was in control of most of his life. He was happy with his job, with his life, and with his support group of friends. He had a sixteen-year-old stepson named Steve. The stepson frequently yelled at William and disrespected him. He came home late, disobeyed rules at home, smoked pot, and was stealing money from the house. He refused to follow rules. This unruly boy would come and go as he wanted, breaking curfew, getting into legal trouble, and not doing his homework. For William, who was always taught to be kind and respectful, this was his first experience raising a boy. Over the course of several months of ECT, William was able to recognize that he suffered from excessive fear. He started to outline where his fear was coming from. He had fear of being a poor husband to his loving wife, fear of being a poor father, losing control of his life, and fear that he was losing control of his mind and body.

It was clear to William that he did not agree with or condone this boy's behavior. William began to identify the root causes of his debilitating fear. He had chosen to enter into a relationship that caused him fear. In therapy, we worked on how to release that fear. We identified and made a list of all of the things that were causing him fear and slowly worked on reducing fear on each one. We also worked on different techniques for reducing stress. One of them was William's love of jogging, which is an excellent for this purpose. When William was running, he felt that he was more in control of his life. Running also helps to oxygenate the blood and improve the circulatory system, as well as the digestive system. It was also a tension reliever for his muscles. Slowly over time, he was able to work on that as a means of stress relaxation. This wouldn't be ideal for everyone but it worked well for William. Why? Because when he jogged his mind was able to daydream and release some of these feelings and sort them out. Yet he still wasn't quite happy and balanced. Things do not always work out as planned. It was only months later, when the stepson Steve moved out of the home, that William felt much calmer.

Take for example a young couple in their twenties who have a child. Instead of being born healthy this child was born with a birth defect or heart defect. The first few years of the couple's relationship is spent at doctors' offices, not sleeping and excessive financial pain. This could be any situation. The point is things change as you go forward. In William's case he sought relief from excessive fear. By utilizing some of the ECT techniques used by all therapists to relieve stress, William had success distancing himself in the same way that Drew had in boot camp.

The difference between William's case and Drew's was that Drew never had to go back to his relationship with stress. Boot camp was over and done. So Drew was able to leave therapy pretty whole. With William, his stepson was still belligerent and didn't want to go to therapy. So as we examine William's situation it was clear that the boy had displayed power over his stepfather from time to time. William felt helpless. For a brief time, William tried to work on parenting skills with his wife and it helped a little bit. William recognized that he had limited power in this situation and he needed to work on his own situation separate from his stepson. What he did to resolve the situation was to spend less time with his stepson.

It was basically rolling the dice. What he was able to do was to peaceably co-exist with his stepson for about a year and a half. Yet he still suffered debilitation stress. When he started therapy his stress was about a nine or ten, but as he worked some of these ways to relax himself such as jogging and releasing his feelings, by talking in therapy it dropped down to about a five or a six. He didn't get completely better until the boy went off to college. Even then William continued with therapy, and he started to become calmer. He tried different techniques to relieve stress. For instance, he was doing more writing, listening to music, and he got a dog and started walking it throughout the neighborhood. Eventually, he was able to lower his stress to a one or two.

William continued in therapy for a year or two. He had other situations arise like health issues, and his stress went up again, but because he did ECT he was able to recognize these fears and reduce them too. Later on, he had more and more fears over some of his business clients who were causing him stress, but once again he was able to use ECT and recognize how his body felt. He was able to process his feelings and move forward and become more balanced. This was a person I worked with for five or six years and he was able to do a marvelous job of monitoring his body, identifying fears and having techniques in place to reduce them.

With Emotional Core Therapy, the client has power to enter and leave relationships. William had spent years as an adult not fully understanding his emotions but he never needed professional help before. Now he was able to monitor his body and his authentic feelings and go on with his life. I would call Williams's therapy successful because he was successful in identifying his feelings, recognizing toxic relationships, making choices to reduce stress, getting over relationships and monitoring his body for symptoms of stress. He did this to a good degree. That's all we can do with ECT. There is no answer or solution to avoid pain. Therapists cannot make decisions for clients. The client has to make decisions about which relationships that they want to enter into. Sometimes people have been in a toxic situation. You have to be supportive within those situations and try to reduce the stress. The relief may not, however, be instant all the time.

This can be particularly true when dealing with on the job stress. As just about everybody knows, workplace stress can be very demanding on one's psyche. Oftentimes an employer will place demands on their employees that cause excessive fear. For years, the medical community would have their trainees, called residents, work 80-90-hour weeks. Often 12-16 hour days. When the demands on a person are this high, anxiety conditions are likely to develop. This is because anxiety is another word for fear. These medical students had increased fear, or excessive fear related to the tasks of their profession. Fortunately for the medical profession, they began to recognize the issue and make changes. What good is a doctor to his or her children and family if he or she has to be gone all day? Residents were experiencing difficulty, not only with their work, but also with their family relationships. How could they not? Their family members have needs also. We discussed in the first chapter that people have emotional, financial, spiritual, and physical needs. If you are gone out of the house all the time, how can you meet the needs of others?

Workplace stress (or school stress) can vary from person to person depending on many factors. Consider a postman or deliveryman. If the person in this job has an injury or condition with his feet and the job requires walking all day, this job would cause excessive stress. What if another individual has no health problems and enjoys nature, being outside, and helping people. In stark contrast, he may love the job. Two different people, same job, yet different levels of stress. That's because people experience stress differently. Still, if you examine the most stressful jobs in our society, most of them cause excessive fear on a normal human's emotions. Look no further than a soldier, policeman, ironworker, professional football player, or a stay at home mother of five, and you will see a common variable. Most of these jobs require a great deal of tasks to be completed, usually in uncomfortable conditions. Thus, they lead to very high levels of stress.

Emotional Core Therapy is about being human and desiring to stay human. That means honoring and processing the four authentic feelings. If an employer causes excess fear in a person that lasts throughout the day it becomes a problem, because it is difficult to transition from denying your senses at work, to honoring them at home. As you are becoming more comfortable with ECT, I hope you are embracing learning ECT off the golf course. Many of us have seen rich, successful, and talented pro athletes in most every sport suffer debilitating stress away from the sports they love. Having a positive and healthy lifestyle on and off the golf course can be an attainable goal that is possible for nearly all golfers once you learn and apply ECT.

List Five Relationships That You Have Entered That Have Caused You Fear On And Off The Golf Course

A) PLAYING A GOLF MATCH IN INCLEMENT WEATHER CONDITIONS

B) GOING ON A ROLLER COASTER.

1)

2)

3)

4)

5)

NOTES:

List Five Ways You Can Release Debilitating Feelings Of Fear On And Off The Golf Course

A) Slow, deep breaths after each golf shot

B) Call a trustworthy friend and chitchat

1)

2)

3)

4)

5)

NOTES:

Symptoms Of Anxiety

Having an increased heart rate

Breathing rapidly (hyperventilation)

Feeling powerless

Having a sense of impending danger, panic or doom

Feeling apprehensive

Sweating

Feeling weak or fatigued

Trembling

List Five Of Your Own Symptoms Of Anxiety On And Off The Golf Course

1)

2)

3)

4)

5)

NOTES:

ECT Flow Chart

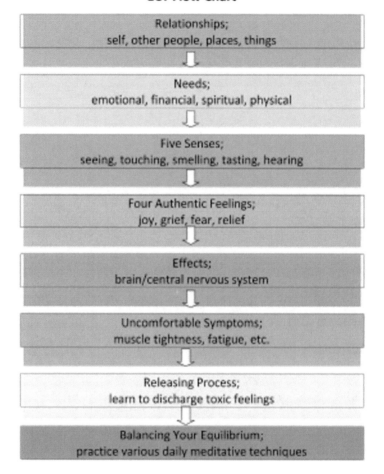

Relationships;
self, other people, places, things

Needs;
emotional, financial, spiritual, physical

Five Senses;
seeing, touching, smelling, tasting, hearing

Four Authentic Feelings;
joy, grief, fear, relief

Effects;
brain/central nervous system

Uncomfortable Symptoms;
muscle tightness, fatigue, etc.

Releasing Process;
learn to discharge toxic feelings

Balancing Your Equilibrium;
practice various daily meditative techniques

CHAPTER FIVE
Anger and other Aspects of the Golf Game

Anger is an important aspect of the golf game that all golfers need to understand how to control. That being said, not all golfers are affected to the same degree by this emotion. Yet nearly all golfers have become angry on the golf course at some time or another. So in this chapter we will address how to not let anger hurt you both on and off the golf course. We will also be discussing other emotional aspects of the golf game. We will talk about how addictions can hurt golfers and also how to keep our support system strong and stable.

The first case I want to mention is about an amateur golfer I worked with named Ralph. He oftentimes was completely unaware of how his anger adversely affected his golf game. Normally an easygoing guy, Ralph was a case I like to talk about because he really benefited from ECT in the short time that we worked together. Although Ralph would get angry at various parts of his golf game, we are only going to focus on one aspect in this chapter. That area is the use of Ralph's short iron clubs when he had an approach shot into the green. Usually, this distance was between a hundred and forty yards and seventy yards. The clubs he had trouble with were his eight iron through his lob wedge. Not every golf shot hit by these shorter clubs was poor. Indeed, Ralph was a pretty solid golfer who had occasional rounds in the high seventies. Approximately once every three to four holes, Ralph would badly miss his approach shot to the green. He would get so upset he would start swearing or yelling. Sometimes, he would throw his golf clubs. His face would occasionally turn red and his shoulder muscles would get tight. These angry emotions would last from five to fifteen minutes or longer. Often they would affect his next golf shot, which was usually a chip or a putt. Sometimes Ralph would be upset for a couple more golf holes. At times Ralph would be so angry that he was no fun to be around.

Working with Ralph, I explained the danger of being angry on the golf course. Anger is a reaction to the authentic feeling of grief. As I told Ralph, one can train your body and mind to get in touch with the core emotion of grief but it takes time and effort. I'm often amazed at how some women are so in touch with their emotions on the golf course and off the golf course when it comes to anger/grief. I've seen many female golfers get in touch with their true emotion of grief versus getting angry at a golf shot. This is the ideal approach to understanding emotions. Even some cultures and religions highlight the dangers of using anger and can get in touch with the true emotion of grief, which is beneath every angry moment on the golf course.

What's the real problem with anger on the golf course? Besides how unattractive it looks to your fellow golfers. For starters, anger elevates the central nervous system. This is rarely beneficial for golfers. An elevated CNS can alter shot making and affects the fluidity and continuity that every golfer needs to repeat a golf swing. Anger is very difficult to react to and learn from as it happens. Let's look at Ralph to demonstrate what I am saying. Ralph badly misses his approach shot to the green and is visibly upset or angry. Why can't he readily use the information his emotions are trying to teach him? Earlier in the book we discussed how the four true emotions act as a compass or navigation guide on the golf course. They are there to help us if we allow our minds to truly learn from them. Well, in Ralph's case of being angry over a poor approach shot, which of the four true emotions (joy, grief, fear, and relief) is he experiencing? The answer is grief. Most everyone playing with Ralph, besides Ralph himself, knows he is sad and disappointed by his golf shot. Sad and disappointed are just words for the underlying true emotion of grief. When Ralph is busy reacting to his golf shots with anger, he is incapable of learning from them! Why? His body and mind won't let him. Ralph needs to calm down and relax but this takes time.

In my work with Ralph I taught him how to not get in his own way. He was letting his anger hurt his golf game because he was not learning from the true emotion of grief. Over time, many sessions in the office, and on the golf course, Ralph and I would focus on decompressing his anger in a quick and comfortable fashion. The first step was having Ralph accept the ECT process. Did he understand how it works? Did he believe in it? Did he have questions on how it works? It is important to clarify the process and be sure the golfer buys into the process. This also takes time. Ralph and I employed some of the same techniques used earlier in the book (chapter three on grief and chapter four on anxiety) to release his anger. These techniques are universally used by many golfers. Another technique we used with Ralph was to hold and rub his shoulders and arms as a way to soothe himself and calm himself down. We would have Ralph repeat the mantra, "calm down and release the anger" while having him massage his shoulders which were tightened by his tension. Another mantra Ralph would say to himself is "what am I losing? What am I grieving?" This allowed Ralph to be pointed in the right direction as far as trying to get at the core emotion. We would try and have Ralph do this before he was to set up for his next golf shot.

Initially, he was not able to do this as he was still holding onto his anger. Over time, he learned to care for himself properly on the golf course and release his anger quickly. Ralph learned to walk his anger off by doing some brisk walking after he became upset on the golf course. This was a way he calmed himself down. Once we were able to get Ralph to slow down his thinking he began to make better decisions. The key point I tried to teach Ralph is to cognitively understand that anger is just sadness. Ralph and I made a list of 25 golf shots that caused him anger. I showed Ralph that every time he was angry he was just experiencing loss. Once Ralph recognized this and understood this for himself, he was ready to change his behavior on the golf course for the better.

As you, the reader, are learning about these various golfers and people in this book, I hope you are reflecting on your own experiences on the golf course and off the golf course. It takes time to learn anything of value. ECT is no different. Let's see if you can pick out the individual steps of the ECT Flowchart for Ralph? Which relationship was new for Ralph? What were the needs of this new relationship? Which senses did he use? What true emotion did he feel? Which part of his body relayed this information to his muscles? What were his bodily discomfort symptoms? How did he release them? How did he relax?

Another golfer I worked with briefly was a local professional golfer named Susan. Our brief sessions focused on her getting angry after missing putts. All statistics for professionals on the PGA Tour are on their website, www.pgatour.com. One can compare themselves to professionals in most any statistical category, scrambling, driving, putting, etc. I encouraged Susan to look at how the professionals on tour did for the category of putting. She was surprised to see that the average professional made less than 50% of his putts from the distance of 10-15 feet in a recent tournament. Susan was angry at how often she missed putts when she played. When we examined and discussed her technique we found she was more than an adequate putter compared to her peers. Technique was not Susan's problem. Her expectations were unrealistic. She expected to make most of her putts inside 15-20 feet. When her putts would sometimes miss, she would pout and whine to herself. Sometimes, this would affect her for her next putt or on the next hole.

Every golfer, including Susan, experiences golf in a different way. One of the most important parts of the golf game is to have a realistic expectation of how you are performing. This sometimes means taking feedback from golf teaching professionals for technique, nutritionists for healthy eating, personal trainers and physical therapists for conditioning, and golf psychology experts for the mental game. Susan just needed a minor tune up in her mental game to get back on track. She was able to grasp the techniques of ECT quickly and regain her old form. Sometimes just shaving one stroke off your golf game every few rounds is the best we can do. As in other areas, beauty is often in the eye of the beholder in golf. If you can feel in your mind and body that something is not right with your golf game, ask questions from those around you with knowledge on how to solve the problem. As I mentioned to Susan, and all the golfers I work with, you have to learn from your emotions to truly be an effective golfer. When you are busy reacting to golf shots with anger, it is impossible to get to the root of the problem. Since anger is a reaction to grief, Susan needed to mourn her losses and get in touch with the grief before she was able to change what she was doing wrong. I told Susan, "If you put your hand on a hot stove and burned your finger, would you do it again?"

"Of course not!" Susan replied.

"Well, then why would you repeat behaviors that were hurting you on the golf course?"

Learning from the grief that underlies every angry outburst on the golf course is essential for any golfer trying to improve his/her game. Let's now transition off the golf course into some real life situations where anger hurts people and hinders them from being emotionally healthy. As I mentioned before, off the golf course mental health care is essential for competitive and amateur golfers alike. Why? Emotions help navigate humans to live a healthy lifestyle and feel empowered. If you are feeling healthy, you will likely get the most out of your physical training, nutrition, as well as building a positive support system for yourself. One of the key aspects of ECT is that it has you take responsibility for all your relationships on and off the golf course. Only when we fully take responsibility for each relationship we enter into, can we grow and learn from them. So far, when we have discussed off the golf course issues, we've mostly been exploring situations where someone has hurt our feelings or harmed us in some way. We will now examine those circumstances in life where not only someone gets angry at us, but we hurt or harm others with anger. This does not mean that we are bad people. Yet, in our humanness, we see that we all have faults in relationships.

There are times when we accidentally or intentionally hurt others in our lives. Examples might be cutting someone off on the highway, speaking out of turn, or skipping to the front of the line at the grocery store when we are in a hurry. All of us do something like this at least once in a while. The difference, however, between an emotionally healthy person and an abusive person is that the emotionally healthy person truly regrets doing the hurtful or harmful act. Why? They know that hurting someone is destructive in nature.

Consider these four very common expressions:

"Treat others as you want to be treated."

"What goes around, comes around."

"Every action has an equal and opposite and reaction."

"To err is human, to forgive is Divine."

Each of these aphorisms is intended to make us see things from the other person's point of view. Moreover, most religions teach and promote the virtue of forgiveness and reciprocity in relationships. For example, "Forgive us our trespasses as we forgive those who trespass against us," is a phrase from the Christian prayer, "The Our Father" also known as "The Lord's Prayer". In Hinduism, people are taught, "There is no ego in a marriage or relationship." This phrase is given as sage advice to marriage partners so that they can give unselfishly to one another. This same sense of fairness and respect for others can be seen using the techniques of Emotional Core Therapy. With ECT we understand that stress (otherwise known as debilitating feelings of fear and grief) is caused by entering and leaving relationships. As we discussed earlier in the book, when we go towards a relationship we like (such as a good friend) there is joy. When we leave something we like (good friend) there is grief. When we go towards something we dislike (heavy traffic during rush hour) there is fear. When we leave something we dislike, there is relief. Since anger is a reaction to grief, what relationship is being stressed? The answer is often the relationship you have with yourself. In the cases you will read in this chapter keep in mind that each character who is angry is really grieving his own sense of loss. We all, from time to time, have made mistakes that hurt others and brought grief or fear into others' lives. Examples might include yelling at your children or siblings, or "blowing up" at your subordinates at work. The difference is that when you begin to honor your authentic feelings of joy, grief, fear, and relief, you become aware of your uncomfortable muscle and bodily sensations that result from stress. This physical discomfort is a signal that something is wrong with a relationship.

With ECT, we recognize that our normal state of being is one of meditation or relaxation. Hence, we become trained to eliminate the debilitating feelings of fear and loss. Anger is a reaction to grief. People who are angry are in fact, grieving and suffering loss. Each individual varies in their intensity and duration of anger. One of the benefits of using ECT is it helps give us a better grasp of authentic feelings, so we can dig deeper and get to the real roots of someone's anger. We must also realize that anger can affect the central nervous system, so it's important especially as we get older to have less stress on the body, and less anger in one's life. By having less anger and stress, your blood pressure can stay calm and your body can be more regulated. Let's take an example of an angry woman to see how ECT can help her better her communication skills and in turn get her needs met.

The woman in this hypothetical case is named Louise. Louise tells her boyfriend Thomas, "You are such an idiot! You leave the toilet seat up all the time because you are a barbaric slob." Of course, Louise's words are harmful and destructive. With Emotional Core Therapy, Louise is taught to honor herself as well as others. A better way of stating her grief at being treated poorly in the bathroom might be the following: "Thomas, I am saddened that you have left the toilet seat up again. I feel a sense of loss of respect when my earlier request to keep the bathroom tidy was not heard." It doesn't have to be these exact words, but something that conveys this sentiment in a similar non-accusatory yet frankly honest manner. Such words would stand a better chance of drawing Thomas into the discussion of cleaning the bathroom. In stark contrast, the angry yelling by Louise is likely going to detract from their relationship and push Thomas away from her. The more authentic that Thomas and Louise can be with each other, the closer they will become in their relationship.

As people become better at authenticating their four feelings of joy, grief, fear, and relief, they can learn to grow their relationships further and better. ECT would be likely to help Louise evolve as a human being. It would allow her to use more authentic words such as loss and grief instead of "idiot" and "barbaric slob." The words loss and grief would help her get more in touch with her inner self. The sooner Louise gets in touch with her core feelings, the sooner she can release them and move on to a healthier state of being. The beauty of ECT is the ability to simplify hundreds of feelings into one of the four authentic feelings. By doing so, one has a much better chance of releasing psychic pain and moving on from the negative state of being. She started becoming more emotionally centered, and when this happens there is less chance to use anger, as anger is a reaction to one of the four authentic feelings. As you learn to live in a more authentic way, honoring your feelings, you become less inclined to need anger as a response to relationships. Why would one use anger as a means of communication when there are far better, less destructive options available?

Our next example of anger is the hypothetical case of a man named Ted, who is a father of four. He walks into the kitchen one afternoon and sees a pile of dirty dishes. Earlier in the day he had asked his teenaged daughter, Kelly, to wash the dishes. So when he walks into the kitchen later in the day he is shocked to see the dishes still lying in the sink. He loudly yells at Kelly, "What the hell are these dishes still doing here! I told you to do them early this morning. Can't you do what you are told?"

Of course, Ted feels terrible later on about what he did to Kelly. He loves his daughter very much and wonders what is wrong with him that he can't control his anger. Using ECT, we examine the situation for the four authentic feelings. Anger is not one of the four authentic feelings, so what was Ted really feeling? Ted had obviously been shocked when he came into the kitchen and saw the dirty dishes still sitting in the sink. His feeling of grief comes from his perception that the dishes would all be cleaned. In his mind he had envisioned walking into the room and seeing an empty sink with the dishes put away. But what he was really grieving was the loss of feeling respected by his daughter. Ted is simply hurt, but does not know how to process his feelings appropriately. Let's examine how

Ted would approach this situation if he truly had a grasp of Emotional Core Therapy and using the four authentic feelings. He might say, "Hi, Kelly, I know you've been busy but I want to discuss with you how I am feeling. I am a bit sad and hurt that you did not follow through with my request to do the dishes."

Which statement is a better style: 1) "What the hell are these dishes still doing here! I told you to do them early this morning. Can't you do what you are told?" Or, "Hi, Kelly, I know you've been busy but I want to discuss with you how I am feeling. I am bit sad and hurt that you did not follow through with my request to do the dishes." Obviously, the second statement would be better. "Sad" and "hurt" are really just names to describe grief.

In the second example where Ted asserts his feelings we have a better chance of drawing Kelly into the conversation. Anger pulls people away from each other and injects fear into the dialogue and it detracts from healthy communication with other human beings. In the long run, Ted will have a much better relationship with Kelly if he can draw her into conversations rather than pull her away by scaring her. Furthermore, in the last chapter we had discussed how fear adversely affects the central nervous system. That is one of the multitude of reasons why very few people respond well to fear in the long run.

Perhaps Louise and Ted never played golf in their life. Why are their cases important to highlight? The mental game of golf is a "Use it or Lose it" proposition! One has to learn to monitor and identify and release the four true emotions hourly and daily or risk losing their importance.

Another way of looking at this is why play golf in the first place? After all, it is just a game. Well, the reasons all golfers play golf is because they hope it brings them joy. Ditto for life in general. Why not live a healthy lifestyle outside of golf and be the best you can be? Emotional Core Therapy is about being human, and staying human. No one is ever so rich or important that they can afford to deny their authentic self.

Over many years of doing therapy, I am constantly reminded of the humanness of all of us. In my private practice setting, I usually don't work with the serious or profoundly emotionally disturbed. Yet I do have clients who come to me with a wide range of mental health conditions. Some clients who seek treatment have been classified or diagnosed in their past as having Attention Deficit Disorder, BiPolar Disorder, Narcissistic Disorder and Obsessive Disorder. Others have sought treatment for self-mutilation issues such as cutting themselves. Some clients have suffered sexual trauma and sexual dysfunction issues. In my experience, ECT can help a broad spectrum of these types of mental health issues. Why? ECT utilizes core techniques that are common to most humans. For example, who has not suffered feelings of loss or fear? Who cannot benefit from learning various relaxation techniques? When would learning how to release feelings be detrimental to a client?

What I have found is that on rare occasions, I utilize several different techniques (not mentioned in the ECT book) for clients who have more severe personality problems. This is primarily because of resistance to change. Oftentimes you need a variety of psychological techniques to help the more resistant client to grow. In many cases, more energy and focus is needed to bring about positive outcomes with clients who are suffering serious mental health issues. Serious cases of depression, anxiety, and anger would likely benefit from a similar approach for the same reason. Any psychological technique that can successfully release emotions is helpful in treatment. ECT is very inclusive of other therapy approaches that can release emotions such as EMDR, EFT Tapping technique, biofeedback, hypnosis, and art therapy to name just a few. Unfortunately, discussing these would go beyond the scope of his book. I would like to point out that common everyday relaxation techniques like yoga and Pilates can be used with ECT to relax.

One of my favorite movies about hope and optimism is "The Shawshank Redemption." The main character in the movie never gave up hope about getting out of prison. His love of life was so strong that he never gave up on his dream to live his life in freedom. His will was so strong that he spent years and years chiseling rock inside his jail cell. I would like our readers to feel the same way about life. Life is so precious, why not live every day to its fullest? For this prisoner it was a life or death attitude and he chose to live – therefore he chose a way to escape out of prison. ECT provides such a path by allowing us to relinquish toxic pain and negative energy. Remember the rudderless rowboat? What kind of rowboat would you prefer to float around in? One with water seeping in the sides and slowing the boat down? Or one that glides effortlessly through the water? Let's look at what happens when one feels guilty? What is the authentic emotion underlying the emotion of guilt? As we learned earlier, guilt is really a form of grief. It comes from mourning or grieving the self in relation to hurting another human being. We all "feel guilty" from time to time. Why? It is human nature to accidentally hurt other human beings. Let's look at this using an everyday example. Accidentally closing (or slamming) a door on someone. Nearly all of us have raced through a door, not looked behind us, and oops, the door gets shut on the next person entering the room. We feel terribly guilty.

With ECT, we become increasingly in touch with our inner self. We learn to honor our feelings. When we honor our feelings, they become much easier to release. The goal of ECT is to release our four authentic feelings when they enter your mind and body. Thus, it gets a lot simpler to cleanse the soul. A clean soul is the only way you can have a rudderless rowboat. If you shut the door on someone, next time you hold the door open. By holding the door open, you eliminate the chance for further guilt (otherwise known as the authentic feeling of grief). One of the beautiful results of learning ECT is that no one gets a free ride in life if they aspire to stay healthy and human. Just as you can't shut the door on people without guilt, you can't kill, steal, or harm someone else, without feeling guilty (having a sense of loss) also. Why? The feelings of loss will stay inside you and not be released. Remember, the key point of ECT is to live in a meditative and relaxed state of being. In order to do ECT properly one has to monitor and release all four authentic feelings on a daily basis.

Being stuck in a state of grief can be very debilitating. Using slang words for this state of being is not hard to envision. We have all heard the phrase to describe a man who has a consistently angry personality: "What an asshole!" If they were describing a woman who is always yelling at others they might say: "What a bitch!" The phase of being angry all the time like someone described as an "asshole" or "bitch" is a very unhealthy state! That's because, not only are they unable to release their feelings, they are also not even being authentic. If they were authentic, they would be able to grieve, which is a healthier place to be emotionally. When you grieve, at least you can move towards a state of eventual peacefulness and tranquility.

Earlier in the book we discussed how you could gauge someone's success in learning Emotional Core Therapy. The more you can learn and acquire the steps of the ECT Flowchart the more confident you will feel about yourself. This book is not about becoming a leader, gaining fame or fortune. Most of the people who assume high levels of responsibility also have high levels of stress (otherwise known as fear). They have excessive fear because they have too many responsibilities and too many tasks. I want my clients to have power, and to be able to handle their responsibilities without excessive fear or stress. ECT allows clients to get a grasp on what they can and can't handle as far as work and family stress is concerned. Oftentimes, when someone is overly fearful or stressed, anger comes out. The more you become comfortable with the ECT process, the less chance you will become angry. That's because you learn to process your feelings better. Since anger is not an authentic feeling anyway, there becomes less of a need to use anger. Emotionally healthy people can express feelings of sadness, just as readily as feelings of joy. The point is, they are being true to themselves, which is precisely what makes them emotionally healthy in the first place.

As we discuss how Emotional Core Therapy can help golfers off the golf course, I want to highlight an important reason why everyone would benefit from using ECT. In doing so, let's draw upon an analogy that I used at the beginning of the book. Consider something as simple as putting on a jacket on a cold and blustery day. Most every child knows that to protect themselves from the cold, one has to put on layers of clothes to keep warm. It is something we all learn at a young age. This is the same dynamic that we are doing with our feelings. Harmful feelings of fear and loss can cause harm and danger to one's body in much the same way that a snowy and wintry day can adversely affect a person dressed only in a T-shirt and shorts. ECT is a form of self-care that has as a desired effect the reduction of toxic pain. The goal of this book is to make the reader so familiar with the process that they can use it anytime, just like one uses a winter jacket.

At the beginning of the book the above paragraph may not have meant much sense to the reader. Why? At that early stage we had not covered any of the numerous relationship topics that cause one stress (debilitating feelings such as fear and grief). Now that we are near the end of the book this analogy makes more sense and really begins to hit home. That's because most of us can relate somehow to the awful stresses of daily life that we have reviewed such as death, divorce, job or financial loss, etc. We have not only hammered home the concept of "relationships causing stress" but we have also provided solutions. In this book we have discussed how ECT can help in the often mentally intense sport of golf. One of the concepts I help golfers understand is that each shot is a separate relationship. Therefore it is important to process your authentic feelings after each shot and remain in a peaceful state before you focus on your next shot. Let's take a look at this for a professional player who is playing a typical hole on a course. He will hit his drive out into the fairway. That is one shot and one relationship. Whatever experience he feels on this shot, he needs to process those feelings. In this case, he is happy with his shot so he has moments of joy. He experiences joy and releases those feelings by looking at the trees and water around him. He gets relaxed again and then prepares for his next shot in the fairway. This time he hits a poor shot into the heavy grass around the green, called the "rough". Our golfer is sad for a few minutes, but learns to release the feelings properly by processing his thoughts with his caddie. He then prepares for his next shot, which is called a chip. His ball lies deep down in the grass so he has some excess fear in his mind prior to the shot. He appropriately pays attention to his feelings of fear and changes his routine to accommodate the tough "lie or slope" of the grass. He then plays the shot and hits a nice shot near the hole. He is quite "relieved" as he now has an easy putt to get his par and do well on the hole.

His relief comes from ending a fearful event or relationship.

In my experience, golfers are some of the most stable professional athletes out there. Why? Golf requires not only power but finesse and a soft touch. The game also is filled with the human emotions of fear and grief every round. You cannot take drugs or be unstable and be a high performing golfer for a prolonged period of time. Whether it is on the golf course, or in any other aspect of life, ECT is about gaining the power and independence to choose a healthy lifestyle. It is a viable solution to fighting debilitating feelings of fear and loss because of its exacting nature. All stress comes from entering and leaving relationships. The root cause of stress is moving towards relationships that we like or dislike. Most relationships require us to meet demands. To keep things simple, we can categorize these into four areas: emotional, financial, spiritual, and physical. Using our five senses (hearing, touching, seeing, tasting, and smelling) we feel one of four ways: joyful, sad, fearful, or relieved. These four feelings can cause our mind and body various levels of discomfort. We have to release these foreign feelings to reach our normal state of relaxation/comfort. Relaxation and comfort need to be reached on a daily basis so we can continually identify foreign feelings (joy, grief, fear, and relief) and deal with them appropriately.

Although the above paragraph is technical in nature, it is important to highlight. That's because some readers are more technical and science based than others. Also, there is a logical sequence to stress and its treatment. Since this book is psycho educational in nature, the reader can go back to this technically written paragraph to gauge his comprehension of the ECT process. Indeed, I purposely wrote this technical chapter near the end of the book to lessen the fear of the reader. We all learn sequential and technical concepts in life to help aid our development.

Examples include a mechanic learning how to repair a motor. A carpenter building a house. A nurse learning how to properly dispense medication. All of the above careers require education and training and rely on learning a sequence of concepts. ECT is no different, and it can be easy to learn. All you need is will and time. A golf psychologist or therapist often acts like a parent figure to his clients. Ask yourself, why do Mom and Dad always remind their children to dress warm during the winter? Protection. You can get sick and be subjected to long-term damage when you are out in the cold for long periods of time without adequate protection. Emotional Core Therapy is my way of protecting humans from the inevitable harm that accompanies the arrival of debilitating stress. Whether you like it or not, you will suffer fear and loss in your life. In fact, most of us will have at least some minor irritation on a daily or weekly basis. Looking at the global economic problems that have evolved over the past few years it is quite obvious that many people have suffered greatly from traumatic states of fear and grief. The real question is why not protect ourselves from this "harmful cold weather" known as stress. It seems to me that the answer is education. People realize that emotional trauma is a national epidemic but no one knows how to fix the problem. When I see the hundreds of psychology books for sale that take an advanced degree to understand, I see more clearly why a solution has not been found. There needs to be a self-help book that every literate person can read. To that extent, I have tried at great lengths to keep this ECT book reader friendly. Even non-readers can comprehend ECT if they have someone that can teach them the process.

In our ECT Flowchart, we see that needs are broken down to four areas. These are emotional, financial, spiritual, and physical. We have organized needs into these four areas because they provide a simple structure for us to understand what causes us stress. There are literally millions of stresses in relationships. To discuss the various needs of ourselves and others would overwhelm the reader. So for the sake of simplicity we break them down into one of four areas.

Let's take a look at how a simple relationship can be viewed in this manner. We are driving our car when a policeman waves us to stop temporarily to direct traffic. In this case, the relationship with the policeman required a physical need to be addressed. We had to stop our trip temporarily before moving on. A relationship with our husband or wife is much more demanding as far as various needs being met. A wife may have many more needs to be met from her husband during the day, including things such as doing the dishes, walking the dog, going to the store, cutting the lawn, etc. The list goes on and on. The four areas of needs being met (emotional, financial, spiritual, and physical) as a step of ECT is really more of a guideline. It is meant to bring a clearer focus of what really causes us discomfort in relationships. Just as we won't spend a great deal of time discussing the five senses (hearing, touching, smelling, tasting, and seeing), we also will skim over the various needs that have to be met in relationships. That's because both happen to us most of the time automatically, whether we like it or not.

Emotional Core Therapy is about being human and to honor one's self, which in turn requires us to honor others. For this reason, we cannot just focus on what happens to our self in a relationship. Inevitably, we have to respond in some form to others too. From time to time, I hope the reader glances at the ECT Flowchart. Over time the flow and sequence of events will become clearer and clearer. Earlier in the book we discussed how ECT can make a thunderstorm feel like drizzle. To explain our analogy we used an example where we discussed how a teacher that supervises four children has an easier task than one who supervises 150. Discussing the four levels of needs (emotional, financial, spiritual, and physical) can be also viewed in this manner. We can usually sort out the millions of various needs required of us by breaking them down into one of these four areas. One of the key points I tell my golfers and all people is that we are all incomplete human beings with unmet needs. We go to school, work, build family and friends to gain support in life to feel strong. At the end of the day, when we learn to focus on our needs, and others' needs, we are well on our way to building a healthy support system. A healthy support system is essential for any competitive athlete, including golfers.

Working in the golf industry, I see many golfers try and drown away emotional pain through food, cigarettes, and alcohol. These addictions can adversely impact a golfer's performance. Making a swing change in golf can sometimes take weeks and months to complete successfully. Some of my clients suffering minor addictions can make great strides in recovery in the same amount of time. Serious cases of addictions can take much longer. The Eight Step ECT process can help with both swing changes and addictions. The following information will show how Emotional Core Therapy techniques can be used to treat addictions. I will give you a modern definition of the word addiction. Addiction: Compulsive physiological and psychological need for a habit-forming substance. The condition of being habitually or compulsively occupied with or in something. For example, someone having an addiction to shopping or fast cars. Addictions come in so many variations that it would be difficult to list all of them, as they range from alcohol to pornography to gambling and just about everything in between.

I like to use analogies when explaining difficult concepts. A good example of someone attempting to find happiness in being addicted to something is like "Fool's Gold". Years ago, people would search for gold only to find useless rocks that looked like real gold but were valueless. Their hardworking efforts were in vain and useless. That is the same feeling people have when they try to escape life through addictions. The escape or rush you feel from being addicted to something will not last. There is always a crash or downturn to being in an addicted state. In Emotional Core Therapy terms, the rush you feel (the state of being addicted to something) can be seen as people attempting to find temporary or permanent joy from their addiction. Instead, addicts always find the authentic feelings of fear and grief. You cause fear and grief to yourself by being an addict because the addictions never last and are often costly emotionally and financially. You often cause fear and grief to others. This may include your loved ones such as family and friends. Emotional Core Therapy can help those suffering from any addiction. ECT starts with a premise that maintains that the natural state of human beings is to have a mindset that is playful, meditative, relaxed and reflective.

That is where love comes from, and it is what gives human beings power. A relationship with an addiction, like all relationships, is something that we enter into by choice. It is up to each individual to remain in their addicted relationship or leave it for good. As we learn how harmful and toxic our addiction is to our health, we will become motivated to make better relationship choices. Also, we will be motivated to want to leave that relationship with the addiction.

Through ECT you will discover that you already have the power within you to overcome addiction. ECT promotes healing by making people understand that they have the power to love themselves, and to learn how to meditate and relax. That means you are not letting go of your will. Rather, you are coming to comprehend the power that you already have within you to begin moving away from the toxic relationship that you have entered into with addiction. ECT allows us to breakdown the emotions associated with the addictive behaviors. We examine what brings us the four authentic feelings, which are joy, grief, fear and relief, and then use ECT to eliminate whatever it is that is hindering our tranquility. What is causing us pain emotionally? What grief are we trying to drown out with our addictions? What fears are we trying to suppress with drugs and other addictions?

ECT offers practical tools for answering all of these important questions and more, which ultimately leads to effective treatment and recovery. Of course, to use ECT successfully, you do need to be open and honest with your feelings, at least with yourself, and for most of us, with other people. Talking with others can help us sort out our feelings. We have to understand all of the relationships that we enter into, including our relationship with addictions. This does not happen overnight, and it can take several months to effectively learn all of the steps of ECT. It's sort of like taking on a new job; you don't understand all of the responsibilities until you've been on board for a while. So understanding the exact nature of your problems can take some time, and discussing it with others is part of the treatment.

Emotional Core Therapy is about learning to continually remind your mind that a relaxed and meditative state is a healthy lifestyle. Day in and day out we are monitoring, identifying and releasing the four authentic feelings, all of which can be numbed or harmed by addictions. Mental health, substance abuse, and addictions are complex issues that can be extremely challenging even for highly trained professionals. I want to remind readers again to notify their family physician for an appropriate referral when you begin addictions treatment. ECT offers a streamlined and inclusive approach for overcoming all sorts of addictions. Not only that, but when you master ECT (and it's a lot easier than you may think) you will see that not only can it help you to overcome addictions, but it can also help you to live a better, more mentally stable and peaceful life in general. Remember, when you learn the ECT process you can transfer what you learn into other sports, or relationship stress in your life.

I want to share with you a case I worked with of a golf professional named Dennis. Dennis lived with his mom and dad and worked long hours at the golf course. When he came to me, he was clearly suffering from substance abuse issues as he would usually smoke marijuana once during the day and almost every night to fall asleep. Dennis and I worked together several times a week, over a period of three months, to learn how to apply ECT as a way to deal with his emotional stress that was spiraling out of control. Dennis' heavy marijuana use was hurting all of his relationships. His golf game was suffering. His girlfriend was feeling neglected. He was sometimes late for work. Dennis would feel sluggish for part of the day. We used several of the ECT techniques discussed in this book to release the toxic feelings that Dennis was experiencing. Since Dennis' addiction problem was primarily off the golf course, there existed more options for treatment. Whether it is using golf psychology or doing therapy in the office, one thing is for sure. We usually don't find a treatment that works the first time. Oftentimes it is trial and error. We try four or five different techniques. This is similar to changing a golf swing. There does not exist anywhere in the world, a golf pro that can come in and fix a golf swing on the very first try for each new golfer they teach.

Usually, the golf pro will try several different techniques such as changing your grip, changing your stance, changing your swing plane, etc, before he finds success. Ditto for the therapist. One of the techniques that really worked well for Dennis was to relax in a hot bathtub while playing relaxing music. He would also read my book for adults, *Emotional Core Therapy*, which highlights in more detail psychology techniques to help off the course relationship stress. Dennis would practice this technique each night. He would also drink water and lemon tea as a way to calm himself down before going to sleep.

Dennis was suppressing his high level of anxiety through marijuana use so one can see he suffered from a combination of mental health and substance abuse issues. ECT helped treat both emotional problems. Emotional Core Therapy was a good fit for Dennis because we were able to apply the psychological techniques of ECT to all of his relationship issues. We spent some time in therapy discussing his anxiety issues and other times discussing his substance abuse issues. Other times we discussed his golf game.

Using the ECT Flowchart, Dennis was able to regain power over his life. Reviewing the flowchart each week was an efficient way to monitor his emotional state. Dennis was able to identify the self-defeating habits that were the root cause of his troubled state of being. By using ECT, Dennis and I were able to identify the reality that using pot to deal with his relationship anxiety was only hurting him. Dennis began to do cardio exercise at the gym to relieve stress. By doing the elliptical machine, Dennis was getting his excess energy out in a more appropriate manner. He began to spend more time outside as well. Dennis was enjoying his new discoveries about his life. He actually began to perform better in golf as he was becoming more aware of his emotions.

With ECT, Dennis was seeing much more clearly that running from his anxiety was a futile effort. As ECT explains, the four feelings are with us on almost every hole. Why keep on suppressing these emotions with marijuana use? They are still going to be there the rest of your life! Both on and off the golf course. I often tell my golfers and other clients, "When one door closes another door or window opens." It is my way of showing optimism and hope to people that are making tough relationship choices along with changes in their lives. To help the reader examine the emotional growth of Dennis in therapy I will again use the ECT Flowchart. By using the ECT Flowchart the reader can see the learning process that entails working in therapy.

Nothing is easy in life that is worthwhile. As the Buddhists say, "Through suffering comes enlightenment." Sometimes working on an individual step of ECT can take weeks or months, depending on the severity of the problem. As we mentioned previously, there are five to six main components of the ECT Flowchart that require work and insight into how to learn. Several of the steps happen to most of us very quickly. Another important point to remember is that some people have knowledge and ability in one or two steps and need help on certain other steps. People have to assess their own ability and knowledge in an open and honest fashion. Therapy can help in that process.

Getting back to Dennis' case, we examined that Dennis' toxic relationship with his marijuana was causing him to become addicted. Step One of the ECT Flowchart was understanding he had entered into a new relationship.

Step Two of the ECT Flowchart was understanding that new relationships require needs to be met. In the case of marijuana use, the physical need of inhaling marijuana was required by Dennis. He would smoke marijuana as a way to deal with his uncomfortable feelings when he was entering fearful relationships. Dennis was fearful of missing golf shots, being a poor golf coach and employee, being a boyfriend to his girlfriend, and going to bed on time.

Step Three was learning that our five senses were involved in recognizing the needs of others. Dennis was able to hear complaints from both his girlfriend and supervisor at work. Dennis was also able to see that his golf swing and golf game was suffering. Also, Dennis would hear from his mom and dad, complaints about over sleeping and illegal marijuana use. Even Dennis' sense of touch was involved as marijuana use slowed down his otherwise powerful golf swing.

Step Four of the ECT Flowchart was understanding how we authentically feel when stress hits us. Any stressful encounter we face on or off the golf course will evoke one of the four true feelings: joy, grief, fear, or relief. In Step Four, the feeling of fear was oftentimes felt by Dennis. Dennis would try, unsuccessfully, to rid himself of this fear with marijuana.

Step Five of ECT is the process of the emotions getting recognized by our central nervous system. This is an automatic step for nearly all of us, including Dennis. His brain would send messages of fear to his muscular and skeletal system.

Step Six of the ECT Flowchart tells us what bodily symptoms occur when we feel stress. Our mind and body recognize our discomfort that fear has upon us. In the case of Dennis, the golf pro, he had muscle tension in his chest, shoulders, and neck. He also felt weak and sluggish from his marijuana use.

Step Seven of the ECT Flowchart is the releasing process. Learning to discharge feelings. Over time, Dennis learned to find quiet time for himself during the day to meditate and relax. He also verbalized his emotions more with his family and me. Especially stressful events that brought him fear. He also began to exercise and take nightly warm baths with music as a way to calm himself down without marijuana use. This allowed him to regain a sense of himself. We revisited earlier times in his life when he relaxed such as playing soccer, tennis, and working out at the gym. When Dennis exercised he was able to let his mind wander and daydream. His thoughts would be free floating and he became relaxed. It is important to note that others may find working out stressful. That is why you have to research each individual's past to see what suits them best.

Step Eight of the ECT Flowchart is to balance your equilibrium. As you can see from reading the case of Dennis and others in this book it takes time and energy to work through tough emotional states. Dennis would use exercising at the gym along with other meditative techniques to self soothe himself. This is all the more reason to be supportive of anyone who is going through a lifestyle change. Throughout our counseling sessions I would have Dennis rate his level of emotional pain. As we made inroads into Dennis' relationship stressors his level of pain dropped considerably. Having clients rate themselves is a great way to monitor their growth in therapy. It is rare I see someone go straight to recovery from a nine or ten to a one. Usually there is some back and forth movement. That is all the more reason to be kind to yourself while you are learning to understand emotions.

Stress will always enter into our lives, both on and off the golf course. Now that you are learning ECT, however, you will be much better equipped to deal with the bodily discomfort that results by using the ECT Flowchart. It's not an instant solution. Rather an ongoing method of learning to live a calmer and more relaxed lifestyle. Whether it is a situation on the golf course that can be addressed in a matter of minutes or even seconds, or a more serious, long-term issue off the golf course that will play out over weeks or months, the approach is exactly the same. By incorporating the principles of ECT into each moment of our life, we become more aware of our feelings and therefore more in control of our own lives. No longer do we need to feel as though we are at the mercy of fate.

As we near the finish line of our book I want to remind the reader again of the character Dorothy in the movie, "The Wizard of Oz". Dorothy went through tremendous fear and grief when she left Kansas for the Land of Oz. Leaving the comforts of family and loved ones can open up a world of emotions for us as human beings. Add on to this, the ups and downs of being a competitive golfer, and one can see the need to find balance and harmony in a golfer's life. Some of these relationships (on and off the golf course) are positive moments for emotional growth. Unfortunately, some relationships end up hurting our emotional well being. The world is a unique discovery for all of us as adults. My hope is that each and every one of us lives life to its fullest. That we carry on all of our pursuits with passion and vitality. Dorothy reminds all of us that family support is a priority in life. Dorothy clicked her heels and repeated the mantra, "There is no place like home. There is no place like home." She reinforces those values over and over in her mind to commit them to memory.

Emotional Core Therapy follows a similar line of thinking. Learn to love yourself and honor your feelings. Be genuine and authentic with your feelings. Learn from your emotions rather than running away from them. ECT teaches us to treasure and respect our unique spirit as human beings. Each human being is a beautiful creation.

List Five Relationships / Events That Have Caused You Anger On and Off the Golf Course

a) Losing a golf match

b) Someone telling you to "shut up"

1)

2)

3)

4)

5)

NOTES:

List Five Ways That Allow You To Appropriately Process Your Anger On and Off the Golf Course

a) I feel sad when I make mistakes on the golf course.

b) I am hurt (another word for grief) that you borrow my money without paying me back.

1)

2)

3)

4)

5)

NOTES:

Symptoms Of Anger On and Off the Golf Course.

Feeling hot and flushed

Racing heartbeat

Tension in shoulders and neck

Feeling agitated

List Five Of Your Own Symptoms Of Anger On and Off the Golf Course

1)

2)

3)

4)

5)

NOTES:

EMOTIONAL CORE THERAPY TEST. Answers are at bottom of test. By doing this test you will allow your mind to have another way to commit the ECT process to your long-term memory. If you are not sure of an answer try and find the answer in the book. This will help you learn ECT. Also, the way to master the ECT approach is to retake the quiz by doing only the answers you incorrectly answered.

1) According to the ECT approach, the four authentic feelings that arise from relationship stress are?

A) Happiness, depression, fear, anger

B) Joy, anxiety, sadness, anger

C) Joy, grief, fear, and relief

D) Joy, fear, anger, grief.

2) The predominant state of a person that has successfully learned ECT is?

A) Happiness and Joy

B) Assertiveness and calmness

C) Tranquility and balanced equilibrium

D) Loving and positive nature.

3) According to the ECT approach, the root cause of emotional stress is caused by?

A) Associating with angry people

B) Suppressing all emotions on the golf course

C) Holding onto anger in your body and mind

D) Entering and leaving relationships that evoke our authentic feelings.

4) According to the ECT approach, the four authentic feelings are?

A) Permanent states of being

B) Temporary states of being

C) Both permanent and temporary states of being

D) Neither permanent nor temporary states of being

5) According to the ECT approach, a healthy mind occurs when?

A) A person allows their mind time each day to meditate, daydream, and relax

B) A person holds onto feelings of grief and fear for several days

C) Learns to focus only on positive thoughts

D) Stays permanently away from negative people

6) The ECT Flowchart entails?

A) Five steps to learning to identify and process emotions

B) Six steps to identify and process emotions

C) Seven steps to identify and process emotions

D) Eight steps to identify and process emotions

7) According to ECT, relationships with ourselves or others usually involve which needs to be met?

A) Emotional, religious, physical, and financial

B) Emotional, financial, spiritual, and physical

C) Emotional, financial, spiritual, and sexual

D) Cognitive, financial, spiritual, and physical

8) The five senses needed to process emotions are?

A) Seeing, touching, feeling, tasting, and hearing

B) Believing, hearing, touching, tasting, and hearing

C) Hearing, touching, smelling, tasting, and seeing

D) Seeing, believing, touching, tasting, and hearing

9) When learning the ECT approach it is important to?

A). Focus on yourself and no one else while you learn the ECT process

B). Focus on rewards and consequences to learn the ECT approach

C). Find a teacher to help you learn the ECT approach.

D). Be kind to yourself and reward yourself to help learn the ECT approach

10) In order for ECT to be of real value, the process needs to be?

A) Available nearby so you can access the ECT Flowchart

B) Taught in most school aged classrooms

C) Taught as part of marital therapy

D) Learned and committed to one's long term memory through repetition

11) ECT emphasizes that stress can come to us hourly and daily. Therefore we need to release these emotions hourly and daily as a learned habit like brushing your teeth. The "cleansing of the soul" is called?

A) Catharsis

B) Internalization

C) Suppression of emotions

D) Reflection

12) Feelings of sadness or unhappiness. Crying spells. Loss of interest or pleasure in normal activities. Fatigue, tiredness, and loss of energy. These are all symptoms of?

A) Anxiety

B) Anger

C) Depression

D) Addiction

13) According to ECT, symptoms of anxiety include which of the following?

A) Having an increased heart rate, breathing rapidly, sweating, and trembling

B) Being angry throughout the day

C) Being assertive with your angry father

D) Losing hope and feeling suicidal

14) Some symptoms of anger are the following?

A) Feeling hopeless and not wanting to be with friends

B) Feeling tired all the time and not being able to sleep

C) Feeling hot, flushed and agitated. Tension in shoulders and neck

D) Not wanting to deal with conflict at home or work

15) According to ECT, anger is a reaction to which one of the four authentic feelings?

A) Joy

B) Grief

C) Fear

D) Relief

Answers. 1) C. 2) C. 3) D. 4). B. 5). A. 6). D. 7). B. 8). C. 9). D. 10). D. 11). A. 12). C. 13). A. 14). C. 15) B.

One of the breakthrough moments for my clients using ECT is learning to apply it to their own lives. Make a list below of ten stressful events in your life both on and off the golf course. Just like we did with Dennis, process each of these events using the ECT Flowchart.

1)

2)

3)

4)

5)

6)

7)

8)

9)

10)

ECT Flow Chart

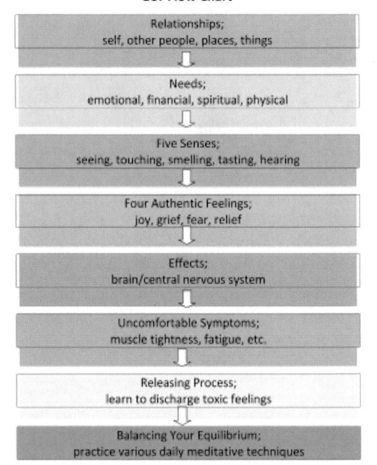

Relationships;
self, other people, places, things

Needs;
emotional, financial, spiritual, physical

Five Senses;
seeing, touching, smelling, tasting, hearing

Four Authentic Feelings;
joy, grief, fear, relief

Effects;
brain/central nervous system

Uncomfortable Symptoms;
muscle tightness, fatigue, etc.

Releasing Process;
learn to discharge toxic feelings

Balancing Your Equilibrium;
practice various daily meditative techniques